Plato Was Wrong!

Footnotes on Doing Philosophy with Young People

David A. Shapiro

ROWMAN & LITTLEFIELD EDUCATION
A division of
ROWMAN & LITTLEFIELD PUBLISHERS, INC.
Lanham • New York • Toronto • Plymouth, UK

Published by Rowman & Littlefield Education
A division of Rowman & Littlefield Publishers, Inc.
A wholly owned subsidary of The Rowman & Littlefield Publishing Group, Inc.
4501 Forbes Boulevard, Suite 200, Lanham, Maryland 20706
www.rowman.com

10 Thornbury Road, Plymouth PL6 7PP, United Kingdom

British Library Cataloguing in Publication Information Available

Library of Congress Cataloging-in-Publication Data

Shapiro, David A., 1957–
Plato was wrong! : footnotes on doing philosophy with young people / David A. Shapiro.
p. cm.
Includes bibliographical references.
ISBN 978-1-61048-618-7 (cloth : alk. paper) — ISBN 978-1-61048-619-4 (pbk. : alk. paper) — ISBN 978-1-61048-620-0 (electronic)
1. Philosophy—Study and teaching. 2. Philosophy—Textbooks. I. Title.
B52.5.S44 2012
107.2—dc23
2011047809

Printed in the United States of America

Contents

Acknowledgments

This book would not have been possible without the participation, first and foremost, of all the young people—kindergarteners through graduate students—whom I've had the honor and pleasure of working with over the years. Their enthusiasm for the practice of philosophy has inspired and sustained me and is the reason that the material I'm presenting in this book exists at all.

I would also like to thank all the classroom teachers who have given me the opportunity to work with their students and allowed me to explore ideas and activities with young people, even though the outcomes have sometimes been unpredictable, and in spite of the fact that my own classroom management skills are still a work in progress.

My deepest gratitude also extends to my colleague, Dr. Jana Mohr Lone, director of the Northwest Center for Philosophy for Children, who not only introduced me to the practice of philosophizing with young people but also has been tireless in securing new and ongoing opportunities for doing philosophy in pre-college classrooms, not just for me, but also for many others interested in having a philosophical dialogue with children.

While I'd been working on this manuscript for a number of years, the final version of the book was prepared during my sabbatical from Cascadia Community College, where I am a full-time faculty member in philosophy. I would be more than remiss if I failed to acknowledge my deep debt of gratitude to my college for providing me with this opportunity, without which this book would still be languishing in manuscript form.

Readers of earlier drafts gave me insightful advice that improved what's here immeasurably. I am grateful to Jana Mohr Lone, Sara Goering, Roberta Israeloff, Thomas Wartenberg, and Joseph Oyler for their comments and suggestions; rest assured that any and all mistakes to be found in these pages were introduced after they'd looked at what I'd written and are, therefore, mine and mine alone.

Finally, I want to thank, from the bottom of my heart, my wife, Jennifer Dixon, and my daughter, Mimi Dixon-Shapiro. Their patience with the philosopher in me, and their abiding love—sometimes in spite of him—is at the foundation of all I do and the source from which the wonder that is philosophy eternally springs.

Introduction

Why Do Philosophy with Young People?

Plato was wrong.

There. I said it, and it felt so good, I'll say it again: Plato was wrong—at least on one vitally important point: the age at which a person should start doing philosophy.

In *The Republic*, book 7, Plato argues that people ought not to begin their study of philosophy—the method of searching for truth known as the dialectic—until about the age of thirty. If youngsters engage in this practice before they are mature, he says, there is a danger that they will develop a taste for arguing just to amuse themselves. They will become skeptical of all that anyone claims to know and, as a result, philosophy will earn a bad name in the eyes of the world.

But he's mistaken about that.

And if the twentieth-century philosopher Alfred North Whitehead was correct and the best characterization of Western philosophy is that it is a series of footnotes to Plato, then the "footnotes" you're currently reading represent my small effort to point out Plato's error.

Rather than waiting until young adulthood, children should begin the study of philosophy at as early an age as possible. Engaging in the practice of doing philosophy—wondering about questions that matter, trading ideas with others involved in that quest, being surprised at having your opinions changed by dialogue and reflection—is so critical to our intellectual and emotional growth that the sooner we do it, the better. And because philosophizing is something that comes naturally to us as human beings, the intentional activity of fostering our innate sense of wonder, of inspiring young minds to ponder big ideas and grapple with eternal questions, most decidedly ought to be a part of education from the earliest grades, if not before.

In schools, I've successfully philosophized with students as young as kindergarten and, as a parent, I happily engaged in philosophical inquiry when my daughter and some of her friends were as young as three or four.

Contrary to what Plato says, this doesn't make youngsters overly argumentative or unnecessarily skeptical. Rather, it tends to encourage them to be better listeners and to develop a taste for meaningful discussion. In my experience, when young people spend time philosophizing together, they develop an increased respect for others' ideas and, just as important, for the reasons that others offer in support of their beliefs. And while the ancient philosopher is right that philosophizing is apt to give youngsters a taste for critical inquiry, this predilection, if fostered in the right way, has positive effects on students and teachers alike, and can only end up improving, rather than detracting from, philosophy's reputation in the world.

The "footnotes" that follow both argue for and illustrate this point. Here you will find a compendium of lesson plans for classroom exercises designed to inspire philosophical inquiry with pre-college students. The work introduces you to a wide range of activities for exploring philosophical questions and problems with young people. Each of the lessons has been used on numerous occasions, and I offer reflections on what teachers who employ these activities with students might expect. There are lessons for a number of topics in philosophy, including metaphysics, epistemology, ethics, and aesthetics, and each is intended to be used in a way that fosters a supportive and caring classroom "community of inquiry," which can be defined as "a group of individuals who collaboratively engage in purposeful critical discourse and reflection to construct personal meaning and confirm mutual understanding" (http://communitiesofinquiry.com/model). I hope that teachers and educators will find these lessons useful in their own classes and can employ them to encourage philosophical inquiry with students they work with themselves.

The story of how these lessons plans were developed and why the practice has convinced me that Plato was wrong as to when students should start studying the "dialectic" begins during the early stages of my own somewhat late entry into the world of academic philosophy.

It took me half a life to complete my undergraduate education. I began college at the age of eighteen, but didn't earn my BA in philosophy until I was thirty-six. At that point, though, I went straight into philosophy graduate school. It didn't take me long to start wondering what I was doing there.

In my second quarter at the University of Washington, right about the time I began to seriously wonder what the point of my studies was and what I was doing with my life (as do most philosophy graduate students at this juncture), I got very lucky.

I was sitting in the office of a professor I was TA-ing for, Ron Moore, and he took a phone call from a former graduate student of his, Jana Mohr Lone, who had recently earned her PhD in philosophy of law. Dr. Mohr Lone, however, had decided not to pursue that line of research but rather was—as I came to glean from what I overheard—in the process of setting up an organization called the Northwest Center for Philosophy for Children, which would bring philosophy and philosophers into pre-college classrooms around the Puget Sound region.

I was somewhat familiar at this time with the philosophy for children "movement" started by Matthew Lipman and the Institute for the Advancement of Philosophy for Children (IAPC) at Montclair State University, having done some reading about it on my own as an undergraduate at the University of Minnesota and following this up with regular volunteer work at schools in the Minneapolis area. And I knew from the angst I was feeling about my own graduate research that what drew me most powerfully to the study of philosophy was classroom teaching, so it was as if the phone call to Professor Moore was actually meant for me.

I soon made contact with Dr. Mohr Lone and became deeply involved with the Northwest Center for Philosophy for Children, an association that has led me, during the past couple of decades, to do philosophy with hundreds of pre-college students, in kindergarten through high school classes, as well as to develop and deliver a university-level course in techniques and strategies for doing philosophy with children.

More importantly, though, my association with the Northwest Center, and especially the opportunities it has provided to do philosophy with pre-college students, has kept alive my interest in philosophy that drew me to the study of the "dialectic" in the first place. Exploring philosophical questions with young people, working together in what we call "a community of inquiry" to wonder together about the sorts of deep questions that have inspired philosophical inquiry throughout the ages, has been, and continues to be, the source of my most rewarding intellectual experiences as a teacher and student of philosophy. Those classroom experiences, challenging and frustrating as they sometimes can be, remain among the most authentic instances of actually doing philosophy that I have ever had. And I think I can say that—in some cases, anyway—students would say the same.

Consequently, I believe that there is real value in sharing what I have learned over the years for other students and teachers of philosophy, especially for those who may be wondering, as I was that afternoon in Dr. Moore's office, what the point of advanced (or, for that matter, beginning) study of philosophy might be. I maintain that the practice of doing philosophy, particularly as it emerges out of exercises and activities such as the ones I discuss in the following pages, has the potential to be uniquely meaningful for both students and teachers who participate in it. Consider what follows as partial repayment on my debt of gratitude for being gifted with the connection to philosophy for children that has meant so much to me over the years.

WHY USE PHILOSOPHICAL EXERCISES?

When I first started doing philosophy with pre-college students, I availed myself of the excellent materials created by the IAPC. I showed up for my initial volunteer session in Mr. Reed's fifth-grade class at T. T. Minor Elementary School in Seattle's Capitol Hill district armed with photocopies of the first chapter from the IAPC's grade-appropriate philosophical novel *Harry Stottlemeier's Discovery* and the superb teacher's manual that accompanies it. I planned to develop and nurture a vital "classroom community of inquiry" using the materials and methods I'd learned in my (admittedly, at the time, somewhat cursory) study of the IAPC's model of doing philosophy for children.

I understood that model to essentially be as follows: Students would read aloud together a work of fiction that raises philosophical questions of one sort or another. They would then generate a list of questions from the text—those questions could explore anything, from specific puzzles about the story to broader, more "philosophical" inquiries. Questions would be written on the board, grouped thematically, and students would choose—typically by voting—which questions they would like to take on. Discussion would then follow, using the questions students had expressed interest in. It would work beautifully; the kids would be fascinated by the text; they would generate long lists of deeply philosophical inquiries; we would ponder at length the meaningful implications of our various perspectives; everyone would listen respectfully to what everyone else had to say; and together we would make progress toward the truth in our shared classroom community of inquiry.

Unfortunately, it didn't quite work that way. The students, most of whom had reading skills below their grade level, really struggled with the text. As they read aloud, their classmates mocked every little slip-up or mispronunciation, making the experience all that more difficult and painful for everyone. The questions they eventually came up with, far from delving into what to my grad-student mind might be construed as "philosophical," were mostly vituperative. "Why is this story so boring?" was one of them. "How come the main character is so stupid?" was another. "Why are we doing this? Can we go outside?" was asked by several kids.

When we finally did get around to attempting a vote on which ones we'd begin exploring, there was a kind of mutiny that resulted in Mr. Reed having to step in and stipulate which question the kids were going to talk about (and if they didn't sit up straight and behave, write about as well), a gesture that, while thankfully having the effect of preventing the inmates from completely taking over the asylum, had such a chilling effect upon discussion that the only sounds coming from the classroom for the next few minutes were the squeaking of chairs and the hemming and hawing of one very uncomfortable graduate student as he tried to make some connection between what we'd just read and Aristotelian logic.

Having had a good deal of experience as a struggling stand-up comedian a few years earlier in my life, I knew all about "flop sweat," but what I'd experienced on stage was a mild perspiration compared to this. I fumbled on for a quarter of an hour or so before Mr. Reed again stepped in and brought the proceedings to a merciful conclusion. He sent the kids out for a recess and, after giving me a moment to gain some semblance of composure, said, "Well, that was interesting. What exactly were you trying to do there?"

I did my best to explain and he nodded respectfully and to his great credit and my eternal gratitude invited me to come back the following week and give it another shot. "But you might want to try something a little different next time, at least at the start," he counseled. "You know, to give the kids some context or something, at least to get them sort of more or less on the same page with you."

I took his words to heart, and so when I arrived the following week, instead of diving right into the text, I started off with a simple exercise ("Word Association," which I describe in chapter 1) that not only was fun but also had the effect of getting the students listening to each other. I next did a short activity called "Are You a Philosopher?" (also described in chapter 1), which interactively helped the kids understand what philosophy and philosophers are all about. The class was lively throughout and, as a matter of fact, we never got to the text at all that day, although we carried on a discussion that touched on a variety of philosophical questions and topics. Students responded to each other—and to me—and Mr. Reed only had to step in once, to help me wind things up, as our discussion went over time and threatened to usurp the subsequent math class.

Flush with the day's success, I made it a point in subsequent weeks to always come prepared with some sort of activity, exercise, or game that would involve the entire class and, with any luck, establish a context for philosophical inquiry. Some worked better than others, but to the extent that an exercise drew the class together and focused us on a question or series of questions that we could explore together, it seemed to me that real philosophy was being done.

One of the challenges I was most eager to meet was to create experiences that would involve all the students simultaneously. In my (again, rather limited) experience with the ideal model of doing philosophy for children, it seemed like a group of about six to eight students worked best. This size allows each child to have a voice when he or she wishes while also making it difficult for anyone to "check out" and avoid participating altogether.

By contrast, Mr. Reed's class had twenty-eight students in it, and many of the classrooms I later worked with were even larger, up to as many as forty in an alternative high school I went to for a couple semesters a few years afterward. In these situations, trying to use a text to facilitate a discussion that would enable all the students to participate—much less participate philosophically—was beyond me. But when we did an activity, one that got everyone involved, I had a good deal more success in drawing philosophical ideas and perspectives from students. And even when the discussions that followed weren't as "philosophical" as I'd hoped they'd be, we'd at least shared an experience among the class that usually helped strengthen our sense of classroom community.

Thus, over the years, I became an inveterate fan, advocate, and developer of classroom activities for doing philosophy with young people. The lesson plans that follow are a result of that. Most are designed to be used with groups of twenty to thirty students, although they can be modified for fewer or, in some cases, greater numbers as well. Generally, they are intended as stand-alone exercises that are meant to foster philosophical inquiry and discussion. In that sense, they function as do, for example, the IAPC's texts. And while, by and large, few are as rich in philosophical depth as Lipman's masterful *Harry Stottlemeier*, some, at least, can be just as successful in stimulating rich philosophical dialogue within a classroom community of inquiry.

HOW ARE THE PHILOSOPHICAL EXERCISES ORGANIZED?

"Philosophy begins in wonder, and wonder is the attitude of a philosopher," said Plato. One of the main goals of doing philosophy with young people is to stimulate and give voice to that natural sense of wonder about the world that exists within us all. Consequently, the emphasis is on questions more than answers, especially at the outset of a class or series of classes.

For this reason, it makes sense to organize each lesson or activity around a question that emerges from philosophical inquiry. This isn't to say that we will necessarily answer that question during the course of the lesson (or even—depending on student interest—take it on directly); rather, it's just that starting with a question has proven useful in organizing lessons and in helping students to grasp the context of questions and topics to be explored. It also helps reduce some of the jargon that tends to make academic philosophy rather opaque and that can, quite frankly, put a quick kibosh on dialogue and discussion in the classroom. Students are more likely, for instance, to be interested in wondering about the question "How do I know what I know?" than they are in taking on topics in epistemology. Similarly, most of us are naturally intrigued by the puzzle "What makes me me?" but when it comes to the so-called problem of personal identity, interest may lag.

With that in mind, the lesson plans that follow are organized under the heading of various questions that have proven to be compelling to students and that, if taken as a whole, do a pretty good job of covering the main "areas" of philosophy, including metaphysics, epistemology, ethics, and aesthetics. And because the question "What is philosophy?" is also a philosophical question, there are also exercises that foster exploration of the nature of philosophy and philosophical questioning as well.

Readers are encouraged to try these exercises out with their own students (or children, grandchildren, friends, relations, colleagues, etc.). And don't worry about whether or not the discussions that follow are adequately "philosophical." Philosophy emerges when thoughtful people wonder together about questions that interest them. As long as you're doing that, you're doing philosophy.

HOW ARE THE PHILOSOPHICAL EXERCISES USED?

The lessons and exercises can be used in a variety of different classroom settings and situations, depending on how the overall curriculum is structured.

Philosophy can be particularly effective if it is integrated in a manner consistent with material that a teacher and his or her students are already examining. For example, a high school computer science instructor doing a lesson about online ethics might use the "Lifeboat Exercise" (chapter 6) to stimulate discussion that relates to topics that the class is already looking into, like computer hacking and online piracy.

On the other hand, if philosophy is going to be done with a class over some time, it makes more sense to work through a philosophy curriculum, touching, if possible, on each of the traditional areas of philosophy in a somewhat structured way. In such a case, that would involve walking through each of the chapters in this book, more or less in the order presented.

By contrast, if the goal is to demonstrate or sample philosophy with young people, a couple of introductory exercises like "Are You a Philosopher?" (chapter 1) or "The Three Questions" (chapter 1) work well and will, with any luck, whet the class's appetite for additional bouts of philosophy.

Teachers may simply try out a single exercise that relates to something they are already examining in their classrooms: the "Hand Dealt" game (chapter 6), for instance, might be a useful complement to a unit on social justice. Or the "Ants and Chocolate" exercise (chapter 6) could support ongoing investigations into animal rights issues.

A teacher leading an ongoing philosophy class might find it valuable to append a number of the exercises found herein to his or her curriculum. For example, he or she could draw from lesson plans in chapter 3 ("What Do I Know?") when exploring epistemology, or from chapter 6 ("What Is the Right Thing to Do?") when doing ethics.

Alternately, the book can be used in sort of a "grab-bag" way. You can just page through until you find something that catches your fancy, and then try it out with students, friends, or family members. It might at first seem to be a bit out of context, but participants will make connections to issues they find relevant and so are apt to relate pretty well to whatever lesson they engage with.

Finally, just a few words about doing philosophy with young people, whether one uses the exercises in this book or employs some other medium to do so.

The most common misstep made by those just starting out is to become overly concerned with ensuring that the experience is sufficiently "philosophical." Often, when adults first go into a pre-college classroom to conduct a philosophy lesson, they feel compelled to present what amounts to university-level philosophical material. This has the effect of not only confusing and boring the students but also, and more problematically, creating a distance between the facilitator and the class, which tends to make the experience passive, rather than active. Instead of promoting dialogue, the lesson becomes a traditional classroom monologue, in which students just sit there, listening (but not really paying attention) to what the presenter has to say.

The most important caveat for folks embarking on the practice of doing philosophy with kids is to refrain from trying to do philosophy. Rather, just think about trying to have an interesting conversation, one that, above all, is of interest to the students. This isn't to say that anything goes. You will want to steer students away from mere story-telling, and obviously personal attacks and inappropriate language are off-limits, but there's really a lot more leeway in what counts as successful philosophizing than one might initially think. The main outcome to strive for is an engaged and engaging classroom community of inquiry. Easier said than done, of course, but the fact that students are communicating with each other matters more than what they're communicating about. Philosophy comes alive via dialogue and discussion; it languishes under the weight of monologue and arcane content.

gue Dr. Jana Mohr Lone, director of the Northwest Center
y for Children, has created a list of tips for leading philoso-
ᵣ··ᵧ ₁or children sessions. With her permission, it is included below. With these tips in hand, you should be all ready to proceed to the lesson plans that follow, and to begin philosophizing with young people on your own.

TIPS FOR SUCCESSFUL PRE-COLLEGE PHILOSOPHY SESSIONS

Things to Do

- Remember that the whole point is to help the students develop their own thinking.
- Let the discussion flow from the students' questions and ideas.
- After reading a story or doing an activity, ask, "What questions did this make you think of?"
- Support the students' building on each other's ideas.
- Show the students that what they say makes you think.
- Encourage the students to speak to one another and not just to you.
- Ask good leading questions in a philosophy session:
  - "What did you mean when you said . . . ?"
  - "That's an interesting idea. Can you explain what you were thinking when you said that?"
  - "What reasons do you have for saying that?"
  - "So then do you agree/disagree with _____'s view?"
  - "How does what you just said relate to what _____ said a moment ago?"
  - "So if what you just said is true, is _____ also true?"
  - "When you said _____, were you assuming _____?"

Things Not to Do

- Tell the students their answers are right or wrong, or give a definitive answer to a philosophical question.
- Allow the students to state their views without giving reasons for them.
- Insist on your own views.
- Be uncomfortable with intervals of silence.
- Permit lengthy discussions of relatively unimportant issues.

- Monopolize the discussion.
- Resolve issues for the students.
- Try to show the students how philosophically sophisticated you are.

LESSON PLANS

The lesson plans are organized around a collection of questions that correspond to the major subfields of philosophy. As mentioned above, depending on how the exercises are to be used, a facilitator might want to proceed sequentially through the lesson plans or pick and choose at will. While there is a general flow from the initial lessons through the later ones, none need really be considered prerequisites to any others. Although there is some context-setting early on, the exercises at the end of the book are meant to stand alone and can be used successfully without having been preceded by those at the front.

Here is a list of the questions covered:

- Chapter 1: What Is Philosophy?
- Chapter 2: What Is Good Thinking? (logic and critical thinking)
- Chapter 3: What Do I Know? (epistemology)
- Chapter 4: What Is Real? (metaphysics)
- Chapter 5: What Is Art? (aesthetics)
- Chapter 6: What Is the Right Thing to Do? (ethics)
- Chapter 7: What Is the Meaning of Life?

At the beginning of each chapter, you will find a brief explanation of the question, along with some general commentary on how it relates to the overall field of philosophy. This is intended to provide some additional guidance as to which exercises and activities a facilitator might want to take on first. Additionally, the final chapter, "Eleven Recommended Readings for Exploring Philosophy with Children," lists readings that have been found to be useful when doing philosophy with children.

Without further ado, then, we turn to the lesson plans themselves.

ONE

What Is Philosophy?

The first question to take on in a philosophy class is the self-referential one: What is philosophy? Students, at all ages, typically come into the experience of philosophy with a variety of conceptions and misconceptions—it's not unusual, for instance, for even college students to confuse philosophy with psychology—and so it's important to begin exploring students' perception of what philosophy is and how it's done right from the start.

Of course, there are many definitions of philosophy, from the "official" one ("love of wisdom") to William James's lovely "Philosophy is an unusually stubborn attempt to think clearly," to Henry Adams's wry "Philosophy: incomprehensible answers to insoluble problems." But in exploring philosophy with young people, the "what" of philosophy is probably not as important as the "how" of it. Our focus tends to be less on *defining* philosophy than on *doing* it. Consequently, getting students involved in the practice of wondering about questions that matter and engaging in dialogue with each other about those questions takes precedence over nailing down an exact definition of the term "philosophy."

Moreover, because philosophy is held in a kind of odd esteem—on the one hand, it's seen as the purest and most exalted of intellectual pursuits (especially by philosophers); on the other hand, it's often (and with some justification) denigrated by people who view it as pointless bickering and meaningless hair-splitting—students tend not to envision themselves as philosophers, or even as scholars capable of doing philosophy. This notion, obviously, needs to be addressed if real philosophy is going to take place in the classroom. Thus, it's useful to begin one's foray into philosophy with pre-college students by taking on those two related issues: What is philosophy, and who is a philosopher?

The following group of lessons can help get both those questions off the ground.

LESSON PLAN: ARE YOU A PHILOSOPHER?

Topic/Question

The Nature of Philosophy/What is philosophy?

Time

About thirty minutes

Materials

A rotary cheese grater works especially well, since it is strange-looking and unfamiliar to many students, but pretty much any item from a coffee cup to a blackboard eraser can be employed

Description

Begin the lesson by asking students a simple question: "When you hear the word 'philosophy,' what comes to mind?"

Phrase the question this way so as not to suggest to students that there is an answer that is being looked for; what's being probed for is what comes to *their* minds when they hear the word. If possible, record their responses on the blackboard as they offer them. It can be quite illuminating to hear what students say.

Typically, one gets responses like "ideas," "arguments," "the way you think about the world." Often, a student will have had some sort of introduction to philosophy and will give the standard definition: "love of wisdom" (although often it's given as "love of knowledge"). It's not unusual for students to conflate philosophy and psychology, and so someone might say something like "Philosophy is the study of the way people think." And especially with high school students, it's not uncommon for a student to say that what comes to mind when he or she hears the word "philosophy" is "dead white males."

Stress that all answers are on the table because in philosophy we want to explore a range of possible responses. It's good to take some time to explore in a little more depth some of the suggestions and try to clear up misconceptions like the conflation of philosophy and psychology, but in general, there's no pressing need to get any sort of working definition of the term; what matters is the sharing of ideas.

This is also an opportunity to help the class begin thinking about thinking—something that philosophy also encourages. As students offer their answers to the question "What comes to mind?" encourage them to think about what's "in their heads" as they respond. "So, we're thinking of our minds," you might say. "What are thoughts?" A related series of questions naturally emerges: "What is the mind?" "What is the relationship between the mind and the brain?" "What does it mean to have something 'on your mind'?"

"Think of an elephant," you might say. "Now you have an elephant on your mind. How big is it? Now think of two elephants. Is the thought of two elephants bigger than the thought of one elephant? What if you think of one hundred elephants? How big is that thought? Can you think of a million elephants? Is there room in your head to do so?"

Thus, students are naturally led into thinking about thinking, a meta-cognitive skill that is not only useful but also mind-blowing and entertaining to students as they begin to engage in it.

Continue in this vein: "Think about it. You're not just thinking now; you're thinking about thinking. It's remarkable the way we can do those two things in our heads simultaneously. Now, notice this. Remember a few seconds ago when you were asked to think about thinking?" (They do.) "Okay, now you're remembering about thinking about thinking. You're doing three things in your head simultaneously! Now suppose you're getting a little confused by all of this. You're being confused about remembering about thinking about thinking. That's four things simultaneously going on in your head. Is there any limit to the number of mental processes you can engage in at the same time?"

Almost invariably, one or more students at this point will say something like "You're making my head hurt!" or "My brain is about to explode." That's great! And exactly what we hope to do in philosophy. (You might also point out that now the student is simultaneously doing five things in their mind: they're being annoyed about being confused about remembering about thinking about thinking.)

Eventually, the exercise continues as students pursue the question "How many of you would consider yourselves philosophers?" If you ask for a show of hands, usually only a few students will raise theirs.

The next step is to present to students a three-part argument in support of the conclusion that they are all philosophers. Here's an opportunity to probe a bit for students' perceptions of the term "argument." Ask, "What comes to mind when you hear the word 'argument'?" You will usually hear things like "fighting," "two people in conflict," "debate," "my little sister," and even sometimes, poignantly, "my mom and dad."

The point can then be made that there's another meaning of the term "argument," and it's one that philosophers like to use. In this case, "argument" simply refers to a way of persuading someone to share a belief that you have. It's a tool for making yourself understood, and it doesn't necessarily imply any conflict whatsoever. With that in mind, students will be presented with a three-part argument to persuade them that they are all philosophers, but that won't involve any fighting or conflict in the process.

The three parts of the argument are as follows: First, students will be shown that they *do what philosophers do*. Second, that they can do it *for the reason* that philosophers do it. Third, that they can do it in the *somewhat special way* that philosophers do it.

So what is it that philosophers do?

Ask students to think of things that they find difficult to stop doing; that is, what do they find difficult to *not* do? Typically, students will answer with responses like "It's hard to stop eating candy"; "I can't stop biting my nails"; "No matter how hard I try, I can't stop watching TV." After each such response say, "Well, let's try." On the count of three, give students the challenge of not eating candy. Presumably, no one in the room will do so. Same with biting their nails or watching TV. Pretty obviously, we *can* stop doing these things, even if it's difficult.

Sooner or later, a student will usually offer up "breathing" as a possibility (or the teacher may prompt this). Again, say to the class, "Well, let's see. On the count of three, everyone stop breathing." It's amusing to observe everyone holding their breath, and the point is made—it's hard to stop breathing, but we all can do it, at least for a little while.

Finally, someone—prompted or not—will say, "thinking." Again, suggest, "On the count of three, everyone stop thinking." You see students doing their best to comply. It's fun to interject something like

"Whatever you do, don't think of a pony," which draws laughter and leads into a discussion of what it was like to try to stop thinking.

Naturally, students will admit that they found it very hard to stop having thoughts; so explore together what was going on in their heads when they tried to do so. Usually, participants will talk about how they attempted to think "don't think" or how they closed their eyes and visualized a black space—which, of course, was a thought they were having. Occasionally, one or more students will claim that they were able to stop thinking; sometimes students will refer to meditative practices that enable a person to suspend thought. All such comments add to the discussion and serve to build upon the main point here—it's *hard* to stop thinking. The point to make is that if you, yourself, find it difficult to suspend your thoughts, then that's the first step to being a philosopher because thinking is what philosophers do a lot of. So reiterate: If you find it hard to stop thinking, then that's step one to being a philosopher.

Continue on to the second point of the argument: You can do what philosophers do (think) for the reason philosophers do it. As an example, tell students something like the following story: "Some years ago, my sister, who was living in a different town than me, was pregnant. She went into the hospital to have her baby and called me up the next day and said, 'Hey Dave, you have a brand-new nephew.' I thought about what she said and could immediately figure something out about that child. What was it?"

It takes no time at all for one or more students to answer that the child was a boy. What's fascinating to probe for is how they know that.

It's quite natural for students—even students as young as kindergarten—to note that since the word "nephew" was used, the child had to be a boy. This typically leads to a discussion about how amazing it is that, as human beings, we can simply think about something—for instance, the word "nephew"—and gain knowledge just by doing so. Point out that what students have done is construct a little argument in their heads that goes something like this: all nephews are boys; this child is a nephew; therefore, this child is a boy. And while that might seem quite mundane, it's really pretty impressive. If you probe to see whether any students are unable to construct such an argument, rarely will you have anyone admit that they are unable to. (Sometimes interesting discussions may arise about whether it's true that all nephews are boys; often students want to wonder if, say, someone's nephew had a sex-change, whether they would be a nephew or a niece.)

The point that follows from this is the second prong of the argument: If you can think to figure things out—and you've demonstrated that you can—then you have two of the three qualities that make you a philosopher.

The third point, then, is to illustrate to students that they can do what philosophers do—that is, think—in the rather special way that philosophers go about it. What follows is an exercise to illustrate this.

Break students up into groups of three to five. In each group, one person is designated to be the scribe; he or she will write down answers that group members come up with.

Hold up a common everyday household item. As noted, a rotary cheese grater works especially well, but pretty much anything—a coffee cup, a blackboard eraser, even a tennis shoe—can be used. Ask students, "What is this thing?" They will typically respond that it is what it's commonly used for; in the case of the cheese grater, the answer given is "It's a cheese grater."

Agree that it *can* be a cheese grater, but that's not all it *could* be. Tell students that you would like them to look at this thing in different ways, from different perspectives, and to come up, in three minutes, with all the different things they can imagine this thing being used for.

Set the groups off to brainstorm their lists. As they work together, have them pass the item around; touching it can help stimulate their creativity. Encourage them to imagine themselves in different settings, and to view the item from different perspectives. "What if you were an ant, what could you use this for? What about if you were a giant? What if you were camping? What if you were an ancient Greek philosopher? What if you melted it down or crushed it?" Remind students not to censor themselves; they should feel free to come up with as many possibilities as they can without trying to edit their answers.

At the end of three minutes, ask the groups to report back. Have them look at their lists and see how many possibilities they've come up with. (As an aside, I usually mention that when I do this exercise with little kids—kindergarten to about third grade—the groups will come up with around twenty to twenty-five different possibilities; when I do the exercise with middle school students, groups usually generate about eighteen possibilities; with high school students, it's more on the order of twelve, and with college students, around ten. So I say, "If you've got about twenty items on your list, congratulate yourselves for reaching the kindergarten level.")

Spokespeople for their groups are asked to share with the class a couple of their favorite uses for the item, which are written on the board or an overhead. (Some of the typical responses with the cheese grater include hamster wheel, paperweight, torture device, pencil sharpener, hair curler, ice crusher, weapon, fashion accessory, and kaleidoscope.)

After all the groups have shared a couple of their favorites, ask the question, "So what *is* this thing?" Point out that you are asking the question quite sincerely. We're not really sure anymore what this contraption is. We're authentically wondering what it is and what makes it so. Students typically offer answers such as "A thing is what it's used for," or "What makes something what it is is what it was originally designed to be," or "It is whatever it does best," or, perhaps most typically, "It is whatever you want it to be."

In asking this type of question, we are doing philosophy. We are wondering, as philosophers do, about the essences of things; we are trying to achieve some sort of clarity about why something is what it is, and what makes it so. This is what we call in philosophy a "metaphysical" inquiry—an inquiry into the nature of reality.

More importantly, we are wondering about something that only a little while earlier seemed commonplace. We took this everyday item—this cheese grater, for instance—looked at it in different ways, from different perspectives, and now find ourselves wondering about it in ways we didn't before.

This is the "punchline," if you will, to this exercise. As philosophers, we commonly take everyday things—tangible things like a cheese grater, or intangible things like ideas—look at them from different perspectives and find ourselves wondering about them. (This is always a good point to interject that one of the most famous of all philosophers, Plato, said, "Philosophy begins in wonder. And wonder is the attitude of the philosopher.")

Indicate to students that if they've gotten even a taste of this—the sense of looking in a new way at something they thought they understood and, as a result, beginning to wonder about it—then they are doing what philosophers do, thinking, in the rather unusual way that philosophers do it.

So then return to the original question asked at the outset of this exercise: "Who here is a philosopher?" Routinely, nearly all students raise their hands this time, which reveals a core assumption of doing philosophy with children. The practice assumes that all people—children especially—are philosophers and that the goal of doing philosophy with kids is to stimulate that natural philosophical impulse within.

Now this, of course, is also open to philosophical inquiry. I've had some very interesting discussions with students about whether indeed all people are philosophers. For example, in one instance, we got into a very rich debate about whether doing philosophy makes a person a philosopher. "I do math all the time," said a student, "but that doesn't make me a mathematician, does it?"

While honoring the process, try to set such concerns aside; the impulse to explore such questions is testament to the philosophical impulse in any case, and so may be evidence in support of the claim I'm making.

What's important is that through this three-part exercise, students tend to be, by and large, persuaded that they are all philosophers—or at least that they have had a taste of what it's like to wonder about things—and this sets the stage for further philosophical inquiry, through additional exercises and activities like those described below.

LESSON PLAN: "ONE RULE" GAME

Topic/Question

The Nature of Philosophy/How do we do philosophy?

Time

About thirty to forty-five minutes

Materials

E. B. White, *Stuart Little* (recommended but not required), and index cards

Description

In order to create what is usually referred to as a classroom "community of inquiry"—a shared space where ideas can be explored in a safe, supportive environment—it's important to establish some rules or guidelines for students to follow. Rather than simply decree these rules, it's preferable to have students generate their own; not only does this encourage them to be more apt to follow the rules, but it also offers an opportunity to begin exploring philosophical ethics before students are even aware of it.

This exercise, therefore, attempts to give students the opportunity to formulate rules or principles that they themselves would choose to be governed by. It explores the norms that they, as a community, would agree upon. And it tries to implement these guidelines in the classroom setting so as to test their viability in the crucible of real-world experience.

Here's how it works: Begin by talking about rules and what their purpose is. To motivate that discussion, it's particularly effective to read together a selection from E. B. White's classic, *Stuart Little*.[1]

In this selection, Stuart—who, in spite of being the son of human parents, looks exactly like (and is the same size as) a field mouse—has taken a one-day job as a substitute teacher. (This is actually a rather interesting metaphysical question: Is Stuart a mouse who was born of human parents, or a human being who looks like a mouse? Sometimes students are eager to take on this inquiry; if so, encourage the discussion. In more than one instance, this has led a class to engage in a focused inquiry into the old "chicken or egg" puzzle. Students have drawn an analogy between Stuart's birth and the birth of the first chicken, and used that analogy to conclude that the chicken had to have come first, just like Stuart's parents.)

In his first moments as schoolteacher, Stuart asks his class what they would like to talk about for the day. He quickly dispatches with the usual subjects—spelling, social studies, and so on—and proposes instead that they talk about the King of the World. One student says that kings are old-fashioned, so Stuart responds that they can instead talk about the Chairman of the World. He allows that he, himself, would like that job; he'd like to be Chairman of the World. The chairman, he says, has to know what the important things are, a quality he believes he has.

Stuart then explores two questions with his students: first, they wonder "What are the important things?" (a shaft of sunlight, a note in music, the way the back of a baby's neck smells if its mother keeps it tidy, ice cream with chocolate sauce); second, they wonder together about what rules should be instituted to sustain those important things. Stuart's students suggest rules like "Nix on swiping anything," "No being mean," and "Don't kill anything except rats." (The last suggestion Stuart rejects as being unfair from the rats' perspective.)

After doing this reading, which is done most effectively as a kind of "staged reading" in which students are assigned characters and recite their character's lines, discuss the pros and cons of such rules, much as Stuart does in his class.

Next, pass out index cards to the students in the class. Ask students to envision a classroom in which they are bound by only one rule. What rule would that be? Students then write down their rules on the index cards.

Some of the rules that students have come up with include the following:

- Don't diss other people's wonders, thoughts, opinions, and questions.
- Raise your hand if you have a question.
- Respect others.
- Don't make fun of others' ideas.
- The class must receive five-minute breaks every hour.
- Respect others' opinions and shut-up when other people talk.
- Microsoft is off-limits for discussion.
- Dave has to bring candy to class every day.

Once students have formulated their rules, collect the index cards and then, after mixing the cards up, pass them back. Each student should now have a rule that he or she didn't write. In groups of two, the students should then work to come to an agreement about which of their two rules they would choose to be bound by.

Depending upon how large the class is, a facilitator might repeat this process with groups of four, having each group of four come to an agreement on one rule out of the two the pair-groups decided upon earlier.

In any case, once the full list of rules has been winnowed down somewhat, write the remaining rules on the board. The class then has to pick five rules that they will choose to be bound by for the remainder of the class. (Let them know, though, that they will always have the option of reconsidering the rules they choose; if good reasons can be given for changing them and the class can agree that changes are warranted, rules can be changed.)

You can change the rules

There's nothing particularly special about the choice to have them agree upon five rules. It has just seemed that five is a fairly manageable number. "A handful of rules" makes sense. Fewer rules than five might not provide enough guidance for the class; more rules than five might be too difficult to remember.

Ultimately, students end up voting for the five rules they prefer; often there is some overlap among the five. For instance, in one class, one rule was "Respect others." Another rule was "Respect others' ideas." This led to a discussion about whether there's a difference between respecting a person and respecting a person's ideas; students in that class thought it amounted to pretty much the same thing. Still, they wanted to keep both rules.

On several occasions students have included a "meta-rule" that goes something like "Everybody has to obey the rules." This provides a fertile ground for discussion of whether such a rule is necessary. One sixth-grade class decided that it couldn't be since—if that were the case—there would also have to be another rule, "Everybody has to obey the rule about rules," and so on, which would be absurd, they said. (Nevertheless, it did lead to a lot of classroom conversation about why *any* rules should be obeyed.)

Sometimes a strange or challenging rule slips in. At a middle school I regularly go to, the students chose as one of their rules "Dave has to bring doughnuts to class." I made it a point to abide by the rule. The next class, I brought a box of doughnuts and we used passing them around as a way to explore ideas of fairness. Once the topic of fairness was on the table, we were able to wonder whether it was fair that I was the one who had to be responsible for bringing doughnuts each time. Some students said that since I was a grown-up, it was fair; others said that it wasn't fair to put such a responsibility for the entire group on one person. By the end of class, the students had decided to modify the rule so that it read, "Some-one has to bring a treat to every class." This went on for a few classes until students got tired of it and the rule was changed to "Students are allowed to bring their own treats to class."

Does allowing students to create their own list of rules to be bound by lead to better classroom behavior? It's hard to say—for two reasons.

First, it's not always obvious what constitutes "better" behavior. If it means that students are more likely to do what the teacher tells them to do, to be obedient, then I'd have to say—based on personal experience—

that it doesn't. When students have designed their own rules, they seem less likely to unquestioningly accept any demands that I make.

On the other hand, they do tend to hold up the rules they've created as standards to adhere to among themselves. It's not uncommon to hear students do a bit of self-policing by saying to someone who's acting out something like "Hey! You're breaking rule number three: respect others." (Of course, they might make this comment while standing on their chairs and leaping around. "There's no rule that says you can't do that, Dave!" they cry.)

And second, it's hard for me to make any claims about "better" behavior in the classroom since, in the classes that I lead, behavior tends to be pretty rowdy. However, students do tend to be respectful of the rules they've chosen to abide by. Even when a class becomes rather unruly, they generally end up being more respectful of each other (at least if that's one of the rules they've chosen).

Finally, there is always something of a challenge when it comes to enforcing the rules: What penalties should there be when someone breaks a rule?

One strategy is to have students develop their own set of punishments for rule-breakers; this has often, however, met with only limited success. One time, for instance, a class decided to have students who broke a rule do the "chicken dance" for the rest of the class. This didn't really work since the students who tended to act out and break rules seemed to enjoy the opportunity to get up and dance in front of their peers. Another class wanted to have rule-breakers sent out of the classroom. I was reluctant to do this since the whole point of rules, as I see them, is to create a community where everyone can feel included.

As a consequence of these challenges, the most practical approach might be to do very little in the way of enforcing the rules. Instead, simply refer to the list of rules if and when things start to get out of hand. Stress that rules can be modified, so that if students are finding the list too constraining (or not constraining enough), the class can work together to create a new list. By and large, though, behavior issues tend not to be a huge problem. Usually, students seem to appreciate having their own list of rules and generally abide by them—with the occasional exception. To that end, it's a good practice to type up the list of rules—or, you might say, principles for doing philosophy—and bring copies for students to keep. Here, for instance, is a list from a recent class:

1. Be respectful of people and ideas.
2. Don't have disruptive behavior, including talking when others are talking.
3. Treat others as you wish to be treated.
4. Don't insult people and ideas.
5. Listen when others are speaking and be open to their ideas.

Having the rules available for everyone and posting them in the classroom may not lead to better behavior on the part of students, but it certainly provides a context for talking about how we want to treat each other, and as such, contributes to the creation of a more effective classroom community of inquiry. Most importantly, it gives the students a sense of ownership of their own classroom and, consequently, a stronger sense of autonomy and control of the learning process, which can't help but lead to a more fruitful educational experience for all.

LESSON PLAN: THE THREE QUESTIONS

Topic/Question

The Nature of Philosophy/What is philosophy?

Age Group

Pre-K to third grade, also high school and college students (With picture books like the one suggested below, there sometimes seems to be a "window" during which they are ineffective. That is, they work well for a specified age group—in this case, pre-readers and beginning readers—and then later, when students are skilled readers, they again enjoy such books, but there's a middle space where students who have some facility with reading more complex books sometimes find such materials too simple and, as a result, tend to reject them. This isn't always the case; it's just something to be aware of.)

Time

About thirty minutes

Materials

Jon Muth, *The Three Questions*

Description

This is a very simple and straightforward lesson, emphasizing the importance of questions in the practice of philosophy. The intended outcome is for students to introspect about philosophical questions they would like to explore in a philosophy course. What's especially useful about this lesson is that it helps students to see that any number of questions can, in fact, be philosophical. Often, students may feel that their own inquiries are not sufficiently "deep" or "profound" enough to be considered philosophy. This exercise helps dispel that concern, while at the same time encouraging students to develop questions that can lead to rich and compelling philosophical discussions.

The lesson simply involves reading to students the illustrated picture book *The Three Questions*, by Jon Muth, which is based on a Leo Tolstoy story. In it, a young boy seeks from Leo, a wise old turtle, the answers to his three questions: "Who is the most important one?" "What is the right time?" and "What is the right thing to do?"

Let students know that the class will be having "story-time," and invite them to make themselves comfortable for the reading. Then read the story aloud, stopping at regular intervals to ask students questions along the way. For instance, there's a point in the story where the boy asks his friends, "Who is the most important one?" Each character answers differently. Pose this same question to students and solicit their responses.

At another point, the boy offers to help the aged turtle, Leo, dig his garden. Ask students to share with the class examples of times they have helped someone in need, how that felt, and whether or not they had an obligation to do so.

At the conclusion of the story, have each student write down his or her three most important questions. Students should then pair up and compare and share their three questions with their partners. Afterward, ask the class to revise their questions as necessary based on their dyad discussions, and finally, ask each student to choose one question that he or she would say is the most important question.

Next, go around the room, student by student, having each say aloud his or her most important question. Encourage students to phrase their responses as "My most important question is . . ."

Although, as a standard practice, the community of inquiry model always allows for the so-called pass rule—that is, any student who would prefer not to speak, at any time, simply has to say, "I pass," and may decline to speak without explanation—it's very rare for a student to not take the opportunity to share his or her question with the group. And it can be quite moving to hear what students have identified as their most important questions. Here, for example, is a list from a recent class:

- What do I want to get out of each day, moment, and ultimately life?
- How can I satisfy others around me while satisfying myself?
- When is the right time to do any given thing?
- How can I be there for someone who needs me?
- What can I do to make someone laugh?
- How can I make myself happy?
- What am I to do with my life?
- How can I help those around me most?
- What will ultimately lead to feeling content with this life?
- Who will I become?
- What do I need to be at my best?
- How do I know I have accomplished my life mission?
- What is the meaning of life?
- Is there God?
- What and who will I become in the future?
- What do I want to be?
- What should I choose to study?
- What is the best use of my time?
- What is the purpose of my life?
- Who are my closest friends?
- How do I live each day to the fullest?
- How does one become their ideal self?
- What's truly of value in this life?
- What is the ideal societal structure?
- Who is the most important person to me?
- What do I need to do for that person?
- How do I need to do this?
- What kind of person, who do I want to be?
- How do I fulfill my goals?
- How do I become happy?

Having each student speak his or her question and allowing everyone to hear what each other wonders about has a twofold benefit: first, it creates a great list of topics that everyone is familiar with for further inquiry; second, and probably more important, it helps everyone see that everyone else is engaged in the practice of doing philosophy. As a result, each student comes to feel that he or she is among peers who are also exploring philosophical questions; this seems to me to be what the essence of a community of inquiry is all about.

Time permitting, the lesson can continue by having the class begin discussing one or more of the questions, either by choosing one that appeals to students or, perhaps, by grouping common themes and pursing the theme under which most of the questions fall. (Typically, this will be something to do with the meaning of life or about what's going to happen to individuals in the future.) Additionally, it's valuable to "bank" the questions for future classes. At appropriate times, the teacher can draw from the bank to foster discussion, especially in cases where a planned philosophy session corresponds to one or more of the questions students have come up with. In addition to connecting the curriculum to students' interest, this also has the additional benefit of reinforcing the key point that philosophy is something that we all do naturally and that students come to on their own, even before studying it.

LESSON PLAN: ENERGIZER ACTIVITY—WORD ASSOCIATION

Topic/Question

The Nature of Philosophy/How is philosophy done?

Age Group

Middle school and up

Time

About five to ten minutes

Materials

A stopwatch or watch with a second hand

Description

At a relatively early point in the practice of doing philosophy, it's useful to have students reflect on what they're doing and on how philosophy is best done. Perhaps more than any other discipline, philosophy makes the study of itself part of the discipline. The question "What is philosophy?" is a legitimate area of philosophical inquiry and one that readily inspires students to engage in the very practice they are interrogating.

A variety of exercises and activities can be used to inspire this sort of critical reflection and, in doing so, begin creating a foundation for philosophical reflection across a wide range of topics, not just those associated directly with philosophy.

Teachers can point out to students that sometimes doing philosophy involves wondering about issues that open outward from the discipline—for example, famous "philosophical" questions like "What is truth?" "What is beauty?" and "What is the meaning of life?" But at other times, doing philosophy involves turning the inquiry inward to wonder about the practice itself with questions like "What is philosophy?" and "How do we do philosophy together?"

The following activity is a very simple exercise intended to provide students with an opportunity to think about that second question and, with any luck, to get a better idea of what skills come into play when we do philosophy in a group. The point is merely to get students listening and responding to one another—which, indeed, is key to effective philosophizing. The activity entails nothing more than word association, but this is a big part of what we do in philosophy: we listen to what another person has to say, and then respond, based on what he or she said.

To set up the exercise, briefly model what is about to occur. Point to a nearby student and say something like "We're going to do a word association game, so imagine that _____ says a word [here, ask the indicated student to do so] and then when _____ [pointing to another student] hears that word, he will say a word," and so on.

As an example, in a recent class, the first student said, "dog"; the next, "cat"; the third, "fish"; and so on. In another class, less typically, one girl started with the word "philosophy," while the next student said, "falafel," and the following offered, "gut-bomb."

Tell students to see how fast they can go around the room, associating word to word. The only rule is that if the facilitator can't see how the words are associated, then he or she gets to stop the game, and the student who made the opaque association has to explain how the words are associated. Advise students not to talk when one of their fellow students is thinking; there's a natural tendency for people to shout out words when there's a lull. Discourage them from doing so since it simply puts the person thinking on the spot and makes it more difficult for him or her to respond.

Pick out a student and say that the exercise will begin when he or she has a word in mind. When that student is ready, begin. It's usually a good practice to point to each student as the word associations go around the room and, sometimes, to repeat out loud the word spoken so others can hear.

Keep the clock ticking, even if you have to stop to ask how two words are associated. A typical example would be a pattern of words in a sixth-grade class that went "cake," "ice cream," "fudge," and then, oddly, "seashore." I stopped the process and asked the student how "seashore" was related to "fudge." He said that whenever his family goes to the seashore, they always stop for fudge.

At the end of the round, when each student has said a word, tell the class how long it took them and ask for suggestions as to how they could go faster. Typically, students will suggest that they simply say the first thing that comes to their minds, or that they work within categories, or that they listen more carefully to each other and not try to predict what the person before them is going to say.

Take those suggestions to heart and do another round; usually, it goes faster this time. Again, ask for suggestions for how to speed up the process; usually, at this point, students want to work together to develop a strategy for all to follow. It's also at this juncture, typically, that the broad categories—food, animals, sports—tend to emerge as suggestions.

Do a third round, and usually it goes even faster; what's more important, though, is that students, at this point, tend to be really listening to each other and working together within some common framework of ideas. In doing so, they are improving their skills in doing philosophy even though the exercise itself is not what one might typically consider philosophical.

After this third round, and some discussion, propose, as a final step, that the class play "Word Disassociation." In this last round, students have to listen to the person before them and say a word that has nothing at all to do with the one before. The point here is that, although usually when we do philosophy we try to build upon what someone else has said, it's also necessary that sometimes we head off in a completely unexpected direction. Philosophy typically proceeds by connections; occasionally, though, it leaps forward via disconnection. In any case, this round tends to be a fairly amusing little exercise, and students come up with all sorts of random responses, but it's also fun to see how difficult it can be to not make connections between words and ideas, especially when that's what you were trying to do previously.

It's not a bad idea to restate the point that although this is a kind of silly endeavor, it does model one of the things we try to do in philosophy, which is to listen to another person and then respond by connecting what we have to say with what he or she just said. Although the exercise itself is quite simple, it has proven to be effective for making that point as well as for helping to get students somewhat focused in a classroom and readier to work together in a philosophical community of inquiry.

LESSON PLAN: BLIND PAINTER

Topic/Question

The Nature of Philosophy/What skills do philosophers need?

Age Group

Middle school and up

Time

About twenty-five minutes

Materials

A blackboard or whiteboard, and blank pieces of paper and crayons or colored pencils for each student to draw with

Description

Frame this exercise by making the point that there are two key skills we want to develop when we do philosophy. These are, first, the ability to communicate clearly, and second, the ability to listen actively. When we do philosophy, it's very important that we learn to express ourselves with clarity, to say what we mean in a way that others can understand. It's also vital that we listen actively; we need to ask questions when we don't understand, to rephrase and restate what others say, and to engage in dialogue with our fellow philosophers in order to advance mutual understanding.

This activity offers an opportunity for students to practice those two skills, communicating clearly and listening actively, in a way that's fun, but that also gives them an authentic taste of what it's like to communicate effectively—and also ineffectively, for that matter.

To start this exercise, pair students up, and then have them arrange their chairs back-to-back so that one of the members of each pair faces the board and the other faces away. The student who faces away from the board needs to have a surface to draw on (usually a notebook), a blank piece of paper, and something with which to draw. A crayon or marker is ideal; since students will eventually display what they draw to their classmates, something bright and easy to see from across a classroom works best.

The explanation of the exercise goes something like this: "This exercise is called Blind Painter. The way it works is that the one of you facing away from the board is a painter, but you are blind to everything except what you are painting. The good news is you have a set of eyes to help you. So I am going to draw a picture on the board and you, the painter, are to try to re-create it. However, you can't look at what I'm drawing; only your 'eyes' can do that. Your 'eyes' will have to describe to you what I'm drawing. You need to keep in mind two rules: first, your 'eyes' cannot look at your paper; and second, you the painter cannot look at what I am drawing. Consequently, you will have to use those two skills I mentioned—communicating clearly and listening actively—in order to successfully complete your drawing."

Note that students should feel comfortable engaging in a discussion with each other, but that they should do so in a kind of "stage whisper" since, with many students talking simultaneously, the room can get quite loud.

Commence drawing a picture on the board. Do so slowly, one or two lines at a time, so that the pairs of students can keep up. Monitor the process to make sure you don't get too far ahead. Any picture is fine, but something simple works best—for example, a little scene with a house and a mountain and a tree—the sort of drawing a small child would make.

When the drawing is completed, make a box around the whole picture to indicate that it's finished. Invite the painters to take a look at what has been drawn and to see how close their drawing is to the original. Ask all the painters to come to the front of the room and proudly display their drawings. Then facilitate a question-and-answer session about what worked and what didn't, and how, perhaps, painters and their "eyes" could do a better job of communicating and listening.

Typically, painters commend their "eyes" for giving precise instructions, especially for describing what to draw in terms of recognizable shapes, like triangles, squares, and easily identifiable objects like clouds and letters. The most common complaint is that their "eyes" gave confusing information in regard to the placement—right, left, up, or down—of items in the drawing. Brainstorm together about how to build upon what worked and improve upon what didn't for the next round.

At the conclusion of this discussion, students get back into their pairs, with the former "eyes" now playing the role of painter and vice versa. This time around, it's interesting to draw a much less easy-to-follow drawing. (Usually, I do a cartoon head, something like Fred Flintstone or Homer Simpson. Unlike the first drawing, this one doesn't have easily identifiable objects like trees and houses. Typically, therefore, students have a far more difficult time re-creating what I've done.)

At the conclusion of this drawing, again invite the painters to compare their works to the one on the board. Ask them to come to the front of the room and again proudly display what they've done. (Without fail, the drawings are more interesting this time around, even though they tend not to look very much like what I've drawn.)

At this point, lead a discussion about why this time around was so much trickier and what could have been done to make it easier for the painters to match the drawing. (Sometimes, a discussion about the nature of art emerges here. I've frequently had students wanting to talk about whether the pieces in the second round—which admittedly look little like what I draw—are, in fact, more interesting works of art than those in the first round.) Often students want to talk about whether or not a painter has "failed" if his or her artwork doesn't match the original picture. Occasionally, some students get very worked up about their drawing (or their partner's) not looking like what the teacher has drawn. From time to time, this can lead to a rich discussion of whether or not it was fair that the second time was so much harder. A teacher might put this up for grabs as a topic to inquire about: Is it fair that some people face harder challenges than others? If so, why? If not, why not? What if facing those challenges leads to superior outcomes (like more artistic drawings)? Would you rather be an expert at something simple or a novice at something complex?

The main thing that comes out of the discussion, though, is the value of communicating effectively. Students really do come to see how what they say can be interpreted or misinterpreted by someone else. The connection to philosophical discussion can therefore be made pretty easily.

The other point that is worth mentioning is that sometimes our best efforts to communicate effectively fail because we don't really have a complete picture of what we're trying to share with each other. This is illustrated pretty well by the second round of the exercise. Because what is being illustrated doesn't really become obvious until the artist is finished—that is, it doesn't really look like the head of Fred Flintstone until the last few marks are made—it's hard for us to communicate what we're seeing. Had a set of "eyes," though, waited until the drawing was done and then told his or her painter to draw a cartoon head of Fred Flintstone, the drawing might have come out much closer to what was put on the board. Students tend to appreciate this point and are able to see the connection to the study of philosophy quite easily. But just in case, it's worthwhile making that point explicitly: Philosophy is like this; sometimes it doesn't make sense until we get to the very end. We have to be willing to "live in the question" and allow the whole picture to emerge. Then, when we're all finished, we can look back at what we've done and understand what it all meant.

Again, having done philosophy even just a couple of times, students will recognize this dynamic and appreciate how familiar it is to the practice of philosophical inquiry.

LESSON PLAN: KEEP THE QUESTION GOING

Topic/Question

The Nature of Philosophy/How does philosophical dialogue happen?

Age Group

Fifth grade and up

Time

About ten minutes

Materials

N/A

Description

This is a simple "energizer"-type exercise meant to get students listening to each other while keeping in mind the importance of questions in philosophical inquiry. It's similar to the word association game described above, but it takes it one step further, asking students to listen to each other and respond in a manner that constructs a coherent sentence — in this case, a question.

To set up the exercise, make sure that students are arranged in such a way that they can more or less all see each other; a circle is ideal, but even if students are sitting in rows, it's helpful if they can all turn so that they can keep an eye on their classmates as the exercise proceeds.

The goal of the exercise is for students to see how long they can keep a question going, one word after another, each word added by a subsequent student. When a student thinks that the question has ended, he or she claps his or her hands, indicating that a new question is to begin.

So, for instance, suppose the first student begins with the word "how"; the next says, "does"; the next, "life"; the next, "begin." At this point, that last student might clap his or her hands to indicate the question is finished. Or, if not, the following student would have to keep the question going, perhaps by adding the word "on," to which a subsequent student might say, "Earth," and then clap.

One guideline to keep in mind, and communicate to students, is that it's not permitted to just add the word "and" to what the previous student has said; students must keep the question going without mere concatenation. In other words, it's not kosher to continue a question like "How did life begin on Earth?" with "and" (presumably setting up a continuing question, something like "and how did it begin on Mars?").

Again, as with the word association exercise, it's important to emphasize that students should listen to each other and refrain from shouting out suggestions to their fellow students. Also, what we're really trying to do is formulate interesting and provocative questions that we'd like to explore together.

Usually it works well to let the exercise run for about ten minutes, depending on the size of the group. It's interesting to see if the class can formulate one single question, although the phrase tends to get pretty silly after about ten or so words.

A facilitator might also run the activity with the goal of formulating two or three questions that the class agrees to explore in more detail. Then the exercise isn't so much about the length of the question, but rather about the quality of it.

In any case, at the conclusion of the exercise, it can be very effective to lead a reflective discussion about what has just happened. Try to steer the conversation around to the question of questions and what makes a given question more intriguing, or more philosophical, than another. This isn't a required part of this exercise, especially if the exercise is being used as an energizer at the start of a class; it has, though, on occasion led to some pretty interesting discussions, especially as students raise questions about the nature of questioning.

As a related alternative to this exercise, you might try doing something similar, only instead of continuing a question, continuing a phrase—ideally, one with philosophical import. My colleague at Cascadia Community College, David Nixon, routinely does something like this, which he spins as a "bumper sticker" exercise. Students use the one-word-at-a-time approach to collaboratively, and in real time, "write" a philosophy bumper sticker. As in the "Keep the Question Going" exercise, they indicate that they've come to the end of the phrase by clapping. In one class I observed, for example, the following bumper sticker unfolded: "The . . . meaning . . . of . . . life . . . is . . . to . . . search . . . for . . . the . . . meaning . . . of . . . life" (clap!).

As with the question exercise described earlier, the main benefit of the activity is to encourage students to listen to each other and respond creatively. It does require a bit more philosophical sophistication (or at least background) than merely continuing a question, but there's no reason one couldn't do such an activity with middle school or older students, just so long as they've had some exposure to philosophical content—even merely two or three class periods.

LESSON PLAN: SENSE AND NONSENSE

Topic/Question

The Nature of Philosophy/How do we make sense of philosophy?

Age Group

Fifth grade and up

Time

About fifteen minutes

Materials

Pieces of paper and pens or pencils for students to write with

Description

This activity is meant to encourage students to wonder about words and meaning and the way in which, as philosophers, we are often called upon to make sense of material that might, at first (or third or even fiftieth) blush, seem nonsensical. The exercise is inspired by a line from *Alice in Wonderland*. During the Mad Hatter's tea party, Alice has been listening to the conversation of the March Hare and the Mad Hatter and is feeling quite perplexed. Lewis Carroll describes it in this way:

> Alice felt dreadfully puzzled. The Hatter's remark seemed to her to have no sort of meaning in it, and yet it was certainly English. "I don't quite understand you," she said, as politely as she could.

So, what *is* meaning, anyway? How do words convey it? What does it mean for a string of words to make sense? And can sentences that seem nonsensical actually, upon reflection, make sense?

Ask students to write down, on a small piece of paper, a grammatically correct English sentence that seems nonsensical—that seems, as Alice thought, "to have no sort of meaning in it." As an example, you might suggest the sentence "My homework ate my dog."[2]

Once students have written their sentences, collect the sentences and redistribute them. (If a student gets his or her own sentence, the student is asked to simply give it back in trade for another.)

Students then read their sentences out loud and are asked to imagine a context in which the sentence *would* make sense. For example, a student named Kyle said that the sentence about the homework could make sense if your homework was to study a live lion. In that case, your homework *could* eat your dog and it wouldn't be nonsensical to say so at all. Another student received a sentence that read, "Purple tastes like Tuesday." She imagined a situation in which every day, at school, you were given a box of colored lollipops that didn't have labels on them. "Suppose it's Wednesday," she said, "and you're tasting a purple lollipop that tastes just like one you had the day before. In that case, you could say, 'Purple tastes like Tuesday,' and it would make perfect sense."

What one hopes students get from this exercise—besides some amusement—is a recognition that sometimes statements that seem nonsensical are, upon reflection, perfectly reasonable. When doing philosophy, it makes sense to keep this in mind.

NOTES

1. I owe the inspiration for this exercise to philosopher/children's book author Claudia Mills, who introduced me to this section of *Stuart Little* in a presentation at a philosophy conference.

2. I also like to use Wittgenstein's example: "It's 12:00 noon on the sun."

TWO

What Is Good Thinking?

One of the aspirations of most philosophy teachers is that their students, by doing philosophy, will become better thinkers. From the days of Socrates onward, philosophers have flattered themselves that those of us who engage in the practice of philosophy will improve our ability to think clearly and critically. Of course, this is very difficult to ascertain, and even defining what good thinking entails proves difficult. That said, there's no doubt that thinking about thinking, which is something that philosophy emphasizes, helps students to become more thoughtful and reflective. The following group of exercises, therefore, is useful in assisting young people in developing their skills as philosophical thinkers. Whether this necessarily translates into, say, better scores on standardized tests, remains an open question. But it's certainly something to think about.

LESSON PLAN: GOOD NEWS, BAD NEWS

Topic/Question

Critical Thinking/How do we reason in philosophy?

Age Group

Middle school and up

Time

   About twenty minutes

Materials

   It's helpful to have pre-made sheets of paper with alternating lines reading "The good news is _____" and "The bad news is _____" (see appendix) but they're not crucial: students can make their own

Description

   One of my professors in grad school, William Talbott, would introduce students to the concept of "dialectical reasoning." Broadly, this is reasoning in two directions, from premises to conclusions, and then backward from conclusions to premises. The basic idea is that when you reason from premises to conclusions, you may arrive at a conclusion that doesn't seem right—even if that conclusion is implied by the premises. At that point, you are entitled to reason "backward," from the conclusion to the premises, examining the truth or falsity of each premise in the argument. While students, by and large, seemed to understand the concept, many, if not most, consider this so-called dialectical reasoning to be something that only happens in philosophy class, as opposed to something that happens in "real life."

   This exercise is intended to help students understand that they engage in dialectical reasoning all the time, that it's something we all do naturally, and that it has applications not only in the classroom but in all arenas of life.

   My colleague David Nixon once shared with me an exercise he did that had students sharing "good news" and "bad news" as a way to encourage them to see both sides of an issue. I drew upon his idea for this exercise, connecting it to the concept of dialectical reasoning and creating a written component that has been effective in getting students to engage in that process.

   To begin the exercise, say a few words about dialectical reasoning, making the point that while it sounds rather technical, it is something that students do all the time, most notably when they notice two sides of an issue, and especially when realizing the good news and bad news about a given situation. As an example, consider an old joke:

A guy goes to the doctor for some tests. He comes back a week later and the doctor says, "Well, I have some good news and some bad news. The good news is, the tests came back and we determined that you only have forty-eight hours to live." The guy says, "That's the good news?! What's the bad news?" The doctor says, "Well, we tried to get in touch with you all day yesterday."

After the groans that this inevitably solicits, a less obnoxious example might be in order, something like "The good news is, our hometown baseball team won yesterday. The bad news is, their star player was injured."

With this basic illustration of dialectical reasoning on the table, we are then ready to move into the exercise.

Pass out sheets of paper on which are pre-printed alternating lines of "The good news is _____" and "The bad news is _____." The paper is filled; there are six or seven of each line, alternating one after another. (If pre-printed sheets are not available, no problem; simply have students write the phrases before each sentence during the exercise. Still, experience has proven that that the exercise works better when pre-printed sheets are used.)

Explain to students that the sheets will be used to do an exercise in dialectical reasoning in which the class will get to see how following a line of reasoning can often lead to an unexpected conclusion—an outcome very much in keeping with the philosophical enterprise. Philosophy, when done as it's supposed to be done, doesn't look for evidence to support a claim we already believe in; rather, when it's done the right way, we simply follow the argument to whatever conclusion the premises lead us to, being quite willing to be surprised by the result.

The way the exercise works, then, is as follows: Students begin by writing one piece of good news on their paper. Emphasize this! Often a student (usually a high achiever) will already be in the process of filling out the entire sheet. Reiterate that students have been asked to merely fill out the first piece of good news; they should go no further!

After all the students have completed writing their first piece of good news, they then hand their paper to the person next to them; that person reads the good news and writes a piece of bad news that follows from it. Again, emphasize, just the bad news! That second student then folds down his or her paper so only the last piece of bad news is visible. He or she then hands that paper to another student who reads the visible piece of bad news, writes an associated bit of good news, folds down the paper so only the good news just written is visible, and then hands it to another student, and so on and on until the paper is completely filled.

Highlight two things while this process is going on. First, students are only allowed to read the one piece of news—good or bad — that is visible; they aren't allowed to unfold their papers and read back. Second, students are encouraged to get up and move around the room to pass their papers around so that the readers and writers get all mixed up; you don't want students passing their papers to the same person every time.

As each paper is completed—it ends with a piece of bad news—have students return them to a pile in the front of the room. When all the papers are turned in, hand each back to its original writer of good news. Students then read the papers and are asked to notice especially the first and last lines and the degree to which they could have predicted that last line from the first.

A good practice is to ask students to volunteer to read their entire sheet aloud and reflect together as a class on whether the first piece of good news and the last piece of bad news are connected or not. Usually, some have a kind of tenuous connection while others seem completely disconnected. The point to make here is that this is what often happens—or should happen—in philosophy. We should be willing to explore the dialectic and see where it takes us, even if to unexpected places.

The exercise tends to be pretty fun, albeit a bit silly. Students routinely use the opportunity to be somewhat inappropriate in what they write, or scatological, or just goofy. It's a good idea to set as a ground rule that no names of anyone in the class can be mentioned, though, so even if students use the anonymity of the exercise as an opportunity to be nasty, no one's feelings will be hurt. (If they do so, a discussion—about how people treat each other differently when they're anonymous, for instance—can ensue.)

Despite the somewhat frivolous nature of the activity, real philosophy is done. Students reflect on written claims and respond to those statements in their own words. They allow themselves to follow an argument where it leads without any preconceived notion of where it's supposed to end up. And they discuss these arguments afterward, looking for connections among the various statements. As philosophers, we hope for such a result in all our discussions.

LESSON PLAN: A LITTLE LOGIC

Topic/Question

Philosophical Logic/How do I reason?

Age Group

Seventh grade and up

Time

About thirty minutes

Materials

Eight index cards and the logic puzzle from J. K. Rowling, *Harry Potter and the Sorcerer's Stone*

Description

The primary outcome of this group of linked exercises is to show students that they are better at logic than they think. As a matter of fact, human beings are naturally good at logical reasoning, so long as there's something meaningful at stake. That is, when faced with having to use logic to figure out something that makes a difference to our well-being, we generally do a pretty good job.

By contrast, the kind of theoretical puzzles that students typically take on in logic classes or to which younger students are sometimes introduced in math education are made difficult primarily because they are so theoretical. When it doesn't really matter whether you solve the puzzle or not, the puzzle becomes much harder. Demonstrating to students that when they need to use logic they can do so with some fluency helps instill in them a sense of confidence and accomplishment that can end up improving their overall skills in critical and logical reasoning.

The following exercise illustrates this point for students in two parts.

First, share with them a fairly well-known example from Cosmides and Tooby that makes the point that people do *modus tollens* much better in real-life scenarios than when doing logic puzzles;[1] second, give students the *Harry Potter* logic puzzle to work through, which brings home the point about our increased proficiency in logic when something meaningful is at stake.

The Cosmides and Tooby example has two parts. Begin by drawing four "cards" on the board, as illustrated in figure 2.1. Students are to imagine that the shaded part of the card can slide over to reveal what's underneath; there might be a circle under it or it might be blank.

Then ask students to consider this claim: *In every case, where there is a circle on the left, there is a circle on the right.* Remind them, though, that they are students, so they want to do as little work as possible. The question they are to answer is this: Which cards need to have the shaded part revealed to test whether the claim is true? They might have to reveal all the cards, or maybe only A, or B, or C, or D, or any combination thereof.

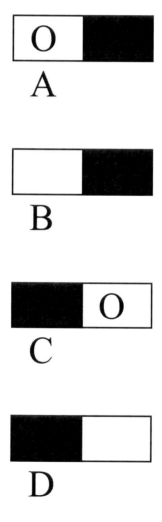

Figure 2.1.

They write their answers down on small slips of paper, which you collect.

Then set up a second example. Get four students to come to the front of the room. Each is given an index card that he or she holds up. The cards read as follows:

1. Beer
2. Soda
3. Over 21
4. Under 21

Now tell students they are inspectors for the liquor-control board who have come to this restaurant to see if there is any underage drinking going on. But as government workers, they want to do as little work as possible, so which patrons do they need to get more information about—related to the patron's age or what he or she is drinking—in order to test whether anyone underage is drinking?

Again, they write their answers down on small slips of paper, which are collected.

Upon examination of their answers, routinely, this is what happens: in the first example, only a handful of students answer correctly (A and D); in the second example, almost all students answer correctly (A and D).

Now ask, "Why is this? After all, both puzzles were the same." (You can fill in this point by demonstrating, on the board, all the possible combinations of each card and showing that it's really only A and D that we would be interested in; the same goes for the beer drinker and the underage drinker in the second example.)

Typically, students respond that the second puzzle was more tangible, that there was something real to figure out, and that since beer was involved, it was more interesting. The first one, by contrast, was just a theoretical puzzle that didn't have anything to grasp on to.

Lead a discussion, then, about how much better we do with logic puzzles when there's something at stake. Solicit examples of problems students have solved with the application of logic. For instance, a sixth grader told me a story about using logic to convince his parents that he ought to be allowed to get a new computer game. They were telling him, he said, that his math grades weren't good enough and argued that if he got the new game, he'd continue to do poorly. "But I pointed out to them their mistake," he said. "Just because *if* I got the game, I'd continue to do bad at math, doesn't mean if I did *not* get the game, I'd do well!" I commended him on recognizing that his parents were committing the fallacy of denying the antecedent, and asked if his strategy worked. "Not exactly," he said, "but once I brought my grades up a little, they let me buy it anyway."

Sometimes students will push back a little on the solution to the first puzzle that both A and D have to be turned over. They will say that you only need to look at A because once you see that there's not a circle on the right, you can stop since the original claim was "In *every* case, where there is a circle on the left, there is a circle on the right." This objection can be used to reinforce the main point of the exercise: When there's something at stake, we all do better at logic. In this case, those raising the objection feel that they've been cheated or duped by the exercise. They are effectively applying logical reasoning to defend themselves against an exercise they think is unfair. Something is at stake—in this instance, their self-esteem or sense of fair play—and, as a result, they're more effective than they would be otherwise in applying the rules of logic.

In any case, the discussion of how much better we do with logic when something matters to us leads naturally into the *Harry Potter* logic puzzle.

Readers of the series will recall that in the first *Harry Potter* book, Harry and Hermione are faced with a challenge in their search for the Sorcerer's (or Philosopher's) Stone. They come across seven potion bottles and have to figure out which one will lead them forward through the fire and which one will take them back to safety. Accompanying the bottles is the following riddle:

> *Danger lies before you, while safety lies behind,*
> *Two of us will help you, whichever you would find.*
> *One among us seven will let you move ahead,*
> *Another will transport the drinker back instead.*
> *Two among our number hold only nettle wine,*
> *Three of us are killers, waiting hidden in line.*
> *Choose, unless you wish to stay here forevermore,*
> *To help you in your choice, we give you these clues four:*
>
> *First, however slyly the poison tries to hide*
> *You will always find some on nettle wine's left side;*
> *Second, different are those who stand at either end,*
> *But if you would move forward, neither is your friend;*
> *Third, as you see clearly, all are different size,*

Neither dwarf nor giant holds death in their insides;
Fourth, the second left and second on the right
Are twins once you taste them, though different at first sight.
(Copyright © J. K. Rowling 1997)

Draw a picture on the board of seven potion bottles, of different sizes and shapes; the smallest bottle is number 3 from the left; the largest is sixth from the left. (With apologies to real artists, my diagram looks something like what is shown in figure 2.2—the solutions written underneath the bottles should not be included in drawing for a class).

Explain to students that with the clues they've been given, they should be able to identify what is in each of the bottles. Then set them to do so.

Usually, a handful of students finish pretty quickly; a good practice is to check their answers and, after confirming that their solutions are correct, ask those students who have successfully completed the puzzle to help students who haven't finished yet. When everyone is done—or has given up—debrief the exercise.

First, ask one of the students who successfully solved the puzzle to show the class how he or she did so. Typically, different students have different methods, and so take some time having students show what they did. It can be informative to compare how some students approach the puzzle very systematically (often a student will construct a grid or

Figure 2.2.

matrix and systematically eliminate options via the clues), while others take a more "seat-of-the-pants" approach. It's worthwhile to explore whether there is a best method or whether whatever works, works.

Eventually, though, a discussion emerges in which the fact that there was something important at stake—in this case, life or death—made students better able to do the logic.

The lesson here is a valuable one, especially for students who tend to think that logic is not their strong suit. Typically, even if students are not convinced that they are better logicians than they think they are, this still leads to an interesting discussion about logic and critical thinking. And the upshot of this is that students tend to be more open to thinking about thinking than they were before, which, above all, is the main take-away of the exercise.

LESSON PLAN: HOW MANY OF THESE DO YOU KNOW TO BE TRUE?

Topic/Question

Critical Thinking/What counts as knowledge?

Age Group

Seventh grade and up

Time

About thirty minutes

Materials

A list of urban legends (see below)

Description

This exercise is designed to get students thinking about what they think they know and, more importantly, how they think they know it. Deceptively simple, yet strangely effective, it involves nothing more than handing out to students a list of claims that "everyone knows are true." Many of these are urban legends of a sort; others are what we sometimes called "received knowledge"—claims that we unreflectively accept as true without really thinking about them. As it turns out, only one of the stories in this exercise is true—the fact that Pittsburgh Pirates pitcher Dock Ellis once threw a no-hitter while under the influence of LSD—but what's interesting to explore is how many of them students will assert and what sort of evidence or testimony they will offer in support of these assertions. (I should note that Ellis reported this in his autobiography, so perhaps this legend's veracity is open for investigation as well.)

To begin the exercise, simply pass out the sheet of claims listed at the end of this chapter and ask students to go through the list by themselves, noting which ones they know to be true. (It's okay if students want to talk to each other some about the claims as they're doing so, but encourage them to decide for themselves which ones they know are true. There will be ample time to come for discussing them together as a group.)

Once students have made their selections, go through the list as a class. Take the claims one by one, asking, for instance, "Who knows the first claim to be true?" As students raise their hands, ask someone to explain how he or she knows it to be the case. Typically, students will respond that "Somebody told me," or "I read it somewhere," or "It's just something everybody knows," or "I saw it on the History Channel," or even "My teacher told me."

List these reasons on the board and continue to probe for other reasons as you go through the list (or some part of it, depending on time limitations). Routinely, students will clamor to know which ones are, in fact, true, but it's important to set this aside until the entire list (or that part of the list that's being taken on) is complete. What you want to emphasize at this point is not whether the claims are true, but how students know them to be. *how?*

In any case, once the list has been gone through, the "spoiler" can be revealed (all but number 10 are false). Naturally, at this point, students will want to know how you supposedly know this. I offer the information about Dock Ellis's autobiography and also admit that I have used the urban-legend website Snopes.com as my research source. So it's possible that I am mistaken about the falsity of some of the claims, but we can talk about that. Usually, we do, and students frequently offer additional support for their beliefs. For example, I've had a student say that her uncle is an insurance salesman and that he told her that insurance premiums are higher on red cars because they get more tickets. Or another assured me that hair does grow back more "whiskery" after shaving because he saw it happen on his own body. The point is not to become dogmatic by insisting on the falsity of any of the claims, but rather to keep wondering together about the sources of our so-called knowledge. This can help provide a natural lead-in to the group of exercises in the next chapter, "What Do I Know?"

How Many of These Do You Know to Be True?

1. The Chevy Nova sold poorly in South America when it was first introduced because in Spanish, *no va* means "no go."
2. New U.S. dollar coins were designed with the motto "In God We Trust" omitted.
3. NASA spent millions of dollars developing an astronaut pen that would work in outer space, while the Soviets solved the same problem by simply using pencils.
4. Slightly overpaying a traffic ticket will keep points off your driving record.
5. Hair and fingernails continue to grow after you die.
6. You can pop popcorn by placing it between certain brands of activated cell phones.
7. The number of people alive today is greater than the number of people who have ever died.
8. Hair grows back thicker or darker or "more whiskery" after it is shaved.
9. Red cars get more speeding tickets than non-red cars.
10. Pittsburgh Pirates pitcher Dock Ellis once threw a no-hitter while under the influence of LSD.
11. We only use 10 percent of our brains.
12. Drinking coffee dehydrates you.
13. A natural sedative in turkey—tryptophan—is what makes you so sleepy after Thanksgiving dinner.
14. Casinos pump extra oxygen into their air systems in the early morning hours so gamblers will not feel tired and want to go to bed.
15. The bulk of donations to Barack Obama's presidential campaign came from wealthy foreign investors.

16. Water in a pan, sink, or toilet rotates counterclockwise in the northern hemisphere and clockwise in the southern hemisphere. This is due to the Coriolis Effect, which is caused by the rotation of the earth.
17. Making yourself cough during a heart attack can help you survive it.
18. In some states, someone caught killing a praying mantis can be punished with a $50–$250 fine.
19. The 9/11 attack on the World Trade Center was an inside job by the U.S. government.

NOTE

1. L. Cosmides, "The Logic of Social Exchange: Has Natural Selection Shaped How Humans Reason? Studies with the Watson Selection Task," *Cognition* 31:187–276.

THREE

What Do I Know?

The area of philosophy known as epistemology deals with the nature of knowledge. And because—at least in the tradition of Western analytic philosophy—something has to be true to qualify as knowledge, epistemology also involves the nature of truth.

This group of exercises explores epistemological questions. Understandably, some of these overlap with chapter 2, "What Is Good Thinking?" And indeed, others include material that might just as easily fall into the first chapter, "What Is Philosophy?" This just goes to show how intertwined the various areas of philosophy are, and how the distinctions among the areas, though useful for organizational purposes, are, to some degree, fairly arbitrary. Nevertheless, when engaging in these exercises with students (even those as young as third or fourth grade), I usually make the point that we are doing epistemology, if for no other reason than to introduce that fancy philosophical term.

LESSON PLAN: "WHAT'S YOUR REASON?" GAME

Topic/Question

Epistemology/Why do we believe what we believe?

Age Group

Fifth grade and up

Time

About thirty minutes

Materials

Pieces of paper and pens or pencils for each student to write with

Description

The intent of this exercise is to get students thinking about how claims are justified and what counts as a good reason for believing something. It's a very simple activity, but one that's proven to be pretty effective and usually a lot of fun.

Begin by asking students to write down something they believe to be true. This can be a perfectly mundane claim like "My name is David" or something with a bit more philosophical "oomph" like "Jesus Christ is Lord." Student then share their beliefs in groups of three, and we talk about those beliefs in the larger group.

Next, ask students to reflect on why they believe those things. Here is a good opportunity to draw a distinction between explanation and justification in epistemology and make the point that, in philosophy, we tend to be more interested in the latter. That is, while students may *explain* that the reason they believe that Jesus is Lord is because that's how they were raised, philosophers want them to set that reason aside and wonder instead about why such a belief is *justified*. To justify a claim means to give reasons for believing it that could persuade someone else to accept it as true. Explanation, by contrast, focuses on describing events or states of affairs that have given rise to a person's own beliefs. Justification falls under the heading of philosophy; it appeals to logic and reason. Explanation falls under the heading of psychology; it refers to personal history and, often, emotion. An example that works for students familiar with popular culture is to use Nelson, the bully character in the television show *The Simpsons*. His awful childhood *explains* why Nelson thinks it's all right to pick on Bart and the other fourth graders; it doesn't, however, *justify* his doing so.

Generally, students come to understand this distinction, although sometimes it's a little muddy. For instance, I've had students wonder whether this counts as explanation or justification: "My reason for believing that my name is David is that everyone has always called me that." I try to deflect such concerns to some degree; the point isn't to always make a hard and clear distinction between explanation and justification, but rather to recognize that such a distinction exists and develop some fluency with it.

In any case, after this discussion, ask students to write down something else that they believe to be true along with three justifications for why they hold this belief. Then break the class into two teams and say that there will be a friendly competition to see how good each team is at identifying claims based on the reasons given for them.

Separate team 1's papers from team 2's and read responses from team 2 to team 1 and vice versa. For example, I begin by taking a page from the stack of team 2 papers. I choose a member of team 1 to be on the "hot seat," and he or she is charged with guessing the first claim from the reasons given. I read these three reasons:

1. Because their hitting is inadequate.
2. Because they aren't willing to spend the money on star players.
3. Because Seattle teams never win the big one.

The claim that these reasons are supporting is "The Mariners won't ever win the World Series." The student in the "hot seat" is allowed to confer with teammates, but he or she ultimately has to take responsibility for the answer. I usually give partial credit. So, for instance, if the student states the claim is "The Mariners stink," I would likely give half a point or so. (For what it's worth, I usually have a lot of fun with the assigning of points; I generally manage to play with the scoring in such a manner as to ensure that the "competition" stays pretty close.)

After the student has given an answer, and a score has been assigned to it, ask team 2 to identify which team member wrote that first example. Take a page from the team 1 stack and ask the team member who wrote that first example to be on the "hot seat." Continue doing this for the rest of the game, always choosing for the "hot seat" the person whose example has just been used with the other team.

Depending on how the game is going, continue through the bulk of the examples, or if people are losing interest, set a score—say, five points—that will win the game. During the "competition," be open to students challenging the scoring as well as raising questions about whether or not the reasons really do support the claim. Again, the point of the game isn't to see who wins, but rather to provide a forum for wondering about the relationship between claims and reasons and what it means for a claim to be justified. And to that end, by and large, the exercise works.

At the end of the game, discuss whether or not the reasons that were offered did, in fact, justify the claims that were made. In other words, if we know just those three things, would we be justified in inferring the claim to be true? This is often a very interesting discussion, as many students want to contend that people are justified in believing whatever they want, whether they have good reason to do so or not. (Of course, we can then wonder whether students have good reason to believe that claim.)

It's fascinating to see how often students will separate what they've just illustrated in the game from what they believe they believe about justification. As a way of probing this further, we sometimes try to come up with the most outlandish belief we can think of and then wonder whether any evidence could justify the claim. To do this, have every student write down on a scrap of paper the craziest claim they can think of. They then trade these papers with their classmates and try to come up with reasons for believing the various claims.

For example, one sixth-grade student a few years back was given the claim "Space aliens have visited Earth" to justify. His three reasons were as follows: (1) lots of people claim to have seen or been abducted by space aliens; (2) the technology of the pyramids in Egypt is too complex to have been invented by humans; and (3) George Bush.

While I wouldn't say I was entirely convinced by his reasons, I was impressed—and amused—by the philosophical thinking that obviously went into his answers.

LESSON PLAN: TWO TRUES, ONE FALSE

Topic/Question

Epistemology/What is truth?

Age Group

Fifth grade and up

Time

About fifteen minutes

Materials

Pieces of paper or index cards and pens or pencils for each student to write with

Description

This exercise is meant to tease out students' intuitions around how knowledge is generated and to get them thinking more generally about what makes a claim true or false. For older students, it can also be used to provide an introduction to the two dominant epistemological themes in the history of Western philosophy, rationalism and empiricism. (Essentially, rationalism is the view that actual knowledge is generated through a process of reasoning alone—champions of this view include Plato and Descartes. Empiricism, by contrast, says that real knowledge comes via experience—Aristotle and John Locke are usually seen as the standard-bearers for this position.)

The way the activity works is quite simple: Begin by asking students to share with the class something that's true. This is a good spot to introduce the concept of a "claim," or a "statement"—that is, a sentence we can assess as either true or false. For example, here's a true claim about me: "My name is David." Solicit other true claims from the class. Students will typically offer up examples like "I am a girl/boy," "Today is [the day of the week]," or "My little sister is a brat." Sometimes a discussion arises about whether a given claim *is* true or not; try to set these aside. The immediate point is that we're interested in claims that are unproblematically true at this point; later, we'll have some tools to better explore the difficult cases.

Next, ask students to share something that's false. You will hear statements like "I am one hundred years old," "I am a boy [or a girl]," and "School is fun."

After we talk a bit about the false claims, write a simple box on the board, and then write inside of it, "The statement in this box is false."

Now ask, "What about this statement? Is it true or false?"

Naturally, students are puzzled. If it's true—that is, if what the statement is saying is true—then it's false, because it says it's false. But if it's false, then it's true . . . but if it's true, it's false, and so on. It's slippery, impossible to get a grip on. Sometimes, especially in higher grades, a student will point out that the statement is paradoxical; almost always, in every grade, one or more students will say that thinking about it makes their heads hurt.

So how do we ever ascertain whether a given claim is true or not? The following exercise gives us some space to wonder about that.

Students are asked to write down on a piece of paper or index card, in no particular order, two statements that are true about them and one that is false. I illustrate what I mean by writing the following on the board:

- I am forty-nine years old.
- I can stand on my head for at least a minute.
- My middle name is Arthur.

When students have written their three claims, say that in a moment they will share them with each other and try to figure out which the false ones are.

First, though, let's reconsider my three claims.

I ask students to weigh in on which of my three claims they take to be false. Typically, most students assume that the second claim, about head standing, is the untrue one. I ask them to explain why this is so. Not surprisingly, students will say things like not too many people can stand on their heads, that I don't look capable of doing so, and that, if indeed I am forty-nine years old, then it's even more unlikely that I can do so.

I then take out my driver's license and have a student read my birth-date; this verifies that the claim that I am forty-nine years old is false. I then point out that I believe I have thus proven that the other two claims are true. I ask students if they are convinced.

Naturally, many students reject the notion that I have proven I can stand on my head simply by demonstrating that the claim about my age is false. "Why?" I ask. "Isn't this a good argument? P1: Two of the following three claims are true; one is false. P2: The claim about Dave's age is false. P3: Therefore, the other two claims are true."

Students will often point out that the first premise in the argument could be false. I assure them that it isn't. Are they therefore convinced that I can stand on my head? No, students will respond. They want to see me standing on my head with their own eyes before they will be satisfied that that claim is true.

Here is a good spot to have a discussion about whether our senses sometimes deceive us and why they think that seeing something is proof that it's true. You can also take this opportunity to explore the question of whether it's the case that just because you've done something, this means you can do it. To illustrate this, I roll up a small piece of paper and throw it to a random spot on the floor. "Look," I say, "I just did that, didn't I? I just threw that paper to a random spot on the floor." I then proceed to throw several more small pieces of rolled up paper at that same spot; inevitably, I am unsuccessful in hitting the same spot. "See? Just because I did that—threw the paper ball at that random spot—doesn't mean I can do it."

"All right," some students will respond. "Doing something once to prove you can do it can just be a lucky chance, like in that example. To be able to do something means being able to do it more than once." This can lead into an interesting discussion about how many times a person has to be able to do something in order for it to be true that they can do it. Twice? Three times? Five? A hundred?

With older students, at an appropriate juncture in the discussion, teachers might want to bring in the concepts of rationalism and empiricism. Hearkening back to my example, the point can be made that those students who want to see me perform a headstand, who don't believe you can establish the veracity of any claim without some sort of sensory experience, are exhibiting sympathy for the epistemological perspective known as empiricism. Those who feel satisfied that my argument proved that I could indeed stand on my head are perhaps more amenable to the perspective known as rationalism. (Typically, the vast majority of students are more aligned with empiricism, although many admit that they just want to see me stand on my head for the fun of it.)

After the conversation has carried on in this vein for a while, ask students to swap their three claims with the student to their left. They must then try to figure out which of the three claims is the false one. While doing so—before their partners tell them which one is false—they are asked to write a few sentences about how they went about trying to determine which claim was false.

Open up the classroom discussion to that question; typically, some interesting discussion ensues. Often, for example, students will note that they figured that the most commonplace claim was likely to be the false one, given that the other student might have been trying to trick them.

Reflecting on this, for example, is thought-provoking. How often, you may ask, do we take the most likely claim to be the false one?

Another means of identifying the false claim that students often cite is something to the effect of "Well, I know a little bit about [my partner] and, therefore, can infer that this claim is probably the false one." This, of course, can lead to a discussion of stereotyping and whether we can draw inferences about people based on some particular aspect of their characters or personalities. Should, for example, we conclude that a person who is forty-nine years old is indeed unlikely to be able to stand on his head for at least a minute?

Still another means is to identify the false claim by reference to oneself. Students will say something like "Well, I would never do [such and such], so I'm pretty sure [my partner] wouldn't either." Not too surprisingly, that approach, as a strategy for establishing truth, is usually only marginally effective. This lends itself to a discussion about individual differences and the degree to which we can assume others are like us. It's delightful to see students have that "A-ha!" moment in which they develop an understanding of each others' individuality. One time, for example, a fifth-grade boy was sure that the false claim of his partner had to be "I hate mayonnaise." "I love mayonnaise," he said, "so that's probably false." When his partner told him that in fact it was true that he hated mayonnaise, it blew the kid's mind. The two of them ended up having a long conversation that stretched well after class about how different their likes and dislikes were. And as a bonus, the pair seemed to subsequently become really good friends, at least for the rest of the time I spent with their class.

One other activity that can evolve out of this exercise is to make it into an informal game. To do this, instead of having students pair off into dyads, split the room into two teams. Collect the claims from each side of the room, keeping them separate. Take one of the left-side students' three claims, designate a student on the right side to be the person choosing the false claim, and then read the three claims. This makes establishing the false claim a little bit more difficult since the person guessing won't know whose claims you are reading. But players will still have to explain why they think the claim they've chosen is false. This opens the discussion up more broadly and also introduces a bit of friendly competition into the activity (teams are awarded a point should the player correctly identify the false claim). The game proceeds by having the person whose claims were chosen try to identify the next false claim as a new set of claims is picked from the other team's pile.

Discussion about strategies for establishing truth and falsity can be introduced as the game proceeds, or can be held off until afterward. (Typically, participants will offer up some of their thoughts about how they tried to determine a false claim, so more often than not the former approach emerges.) Sometimes teams get fairly focused on winning the game and may even call into question whether the false claim of a member of the other team really is false. One student, for instance, insisted that the claim "I've never eaten meat" had to be false, even though his counterpart on the other team said it was true. "If you've ever even licked a stamp," he said, "you've eaten meat." We never ended up establishing whether this was true or false, but we did have a great discussion about whether you can unintentionally lie.

In any case, the main point to explore in the exercise, whether it's done as a game or as a "shared-pair" exercise, is how we go about establishing the truth or falsity of various claims. At the conclusion of the discussion, with younger students, it works well to do a fill-in-the-blank "poem" like this: "One thing that will always be true about me is _____."

Finally, it can be useful, especially with older students, for the students to do some writing about what strategies they typically employ to determine whether a claim is true or false, and whether their own intuitions tend more toward rationalism or empiricism. Doing so can then set up an effective segue into the "Egg Drop" game below, which builds upon similar concepts.

LESSON PLAN: THE "EGG DROP" GAME

Topic/Question

Epistemology/How do we reason empirically?

Age Group

Fifth grade and up

Time

About an hour

Materials

A hardboiled egg, a "blown" egg, sufficient uncooked eggs for every team of two or three students to have one, enough bendy straws for each team of students to have ten, masking tape, scissors, paper towels, and a big garbage bag for clean-up

Description

The idea for this exercise emerges from Wesley Salmon's widely anthologized piece "An Encounter with David Hume," in which Salmon introduces what he calls "Hume's bombshell."[1] Essentially, this is the observation that since the entire scientific method is based on making predictions about future events from past experience, and since, as Hume famously points out, we can never be certain that the future will behave as the past has done, then, in a very real sense, all scientific reasoning is contingent at best, if not downright fallacious.

The intent of this exercise is to get students pondering empirical reasoning in general and to have them begin raising questions about whether it does make sense to make claims about what is going to happen from what has happened. In other words, is it reasonable to predict future events from past experience, even if the outcomes of those events are not necessarily certain?

To really capture students' attention, begin the exercise by climbing on a chair and holding an uncooked egg above some sort of receptacle on the floor (a rectangular baking dish works great). Ask, "What will happen when I drop this egg?" Someone will answer, "It's going to break!" Follow up with "How do you know?" "Because I've dropped eggs in the past and they've always broken" is the standard response. Say, "Well, let's see," and drop the egg. Of course, it breaks.

Point out to the class that what they have just seen is an example of what we could call inductive—empirical—reasoning: drawing conclusions about future events from past experience. Remind them (if the Salmon article has been referenced) that this is what Hume says we can never be certain of. But what are the implications of this? Does it mean that we're never justified in reasoning inductively? Encourage students to talk about this and then suggest that this assumption can be tested.

Climb back on the chair and now hold the hardboiled egg over your head (don't let on that it's hardboiled). Ask, "What will happen when I drop this?" Students will say, "It will break." "How do you know?" "Because we've seen it happen before." "Good! Does having seen it happen once make you more certain that it will happen again?" In general, students reply that it does, although usually one or more may want to press you on whether the egg is hardboiled, an inquiry to deflect at this point.

In any case, when the hardboiled egg is dropped, it doesn't break like the first one did. This usually inspires a discussion about whether or not it was reasonable, based on past experience, to believe that the egg would break, which gets the class deeper into the philosophical question under examination. Most students will say that it still made sense to assume that the egg would break, even if we couldn't be certain about it. It's not like it was an outlandish assumption, such as believing that the egg would float when dropped. So as long as there is pretty good reason to make the inference, the inference is reasonable.

Finally, climb back on the chair and hold up the blown egg: "What will happen now?" "Is it hardboiled?" students inevitably ask, and you can truthfully reply that it isn't. "Well then, it will break," they answer with assurance. "Let's see." Of course, this egg, upon being dropped, falls gently, and while it may crack, it rarely really breaks. Once again, this opens the door to a discussion about whether we are justified in reasoning inductively, given the uncertainty of future outcomes.

As this discussion winds down, segue into the point that, as a matter of fact, we are pretty good at making predictions about what's going to happen, even if the philosophical foundation of such claims is rather sketchy. The exercise we are about to engage in is meant to demonstrate this and to help us reflect upon how good (or bad) we are at reasoning inductively.

Students are divided up into teams of two or three. (Four is acceptable, but less than ideal, since it usually means that at least one team member either gets left out or checks out.)

Teams are told that they have a task set before them, which is to build a device that will protect an uncooked egg from breaking when the egg is dropped from a height of about eight feet. The only items they can use, however, to build their device are those that are provided to them.

Pass out to each group ten flexible straws and about two yards of masking tape. Make as many pairs of scissors available as possible. Teams now have half an hour to build their contraption. They can cut their straws and tape. They can build an egg "catcher" or an egg "protector." The only rule is that they are limited to the supplies they have received.

At the end of the allotted time, each group must make a brief presentation to the class. In it, they must share with the class the name of their contraption and give an argument, using inductive reasoning, as to why they think their device will succeed (or fail).

Some teams like to have their egg to work with—especially, for instance, if they are building a protector around it—so it's fine to give eggs to groups to work with. However, advise them strongly not to break their eggs during development of their contraption: groups will only get one egg to work with. (Sometimes, if I have an extra, I'll break this rule, but it's important to impress upon students the importance of taking care while they work, and also to have paper towels handy should an accident occur.)

When all the groups have finished making their contraption, each group gives their short presentation, including the arguments about why the device will succeed (or fail). Place all the contraptions on a table where everyone can see them. Then, as a class, vote on which devices students think will be most successful (each student can only vote for one device) as well as which devices they think will be least successful. By adding the positive votes up and subtracting the negatives for each device, you can create a list, from lowest to highest score, predicting which devices students think will be least and most successful.

Now, based on the rankings, the class can see how well they are able to predict future events from past experience. Presumably, the devices that have been predicted to fail should fail, and the ones predicted to succeed should succeed—at least, that's what our confidence in the ability to reason inductively depends upon.

Proceed then, by turns, to drop or employ each device, starting with the one the class has said will be least successful. Hilarity ensues—and many paper towels are employed in the clean-up. Typically, if an egg survives the initial fall, the successful device is placed aside for a second or even third drop from some higher spot. (At Cascadia Community College, where I teach, we often use a third-floor balcony with a drop to the sidewalk below for devices successful in previous drops.)

In any case, once all the devices have been dropped or employed, the class can revisit the initial question about inductive reasoning. How well did we do? That is, how many of the devices that we predicted would succeed, did succeed? What about the ones that we predicted would fail? What does this say about our ability to predict future events from past experience?

Usually, our predictions tend to be fairly reliable, but there will also be some anomalies. For instance, a contraption deemed to be ineffective will succeed heroically, or vice versa (one expected to do well will fail on its first attempt). Again, this provides lots of opportunities for thinking and talking about inductive reasoning and succeeds in providing a fun and engaging forum for doing so.

Admittedly, it's not uncommon for some of the subtler "philosophical" points to be overwhelmed by the overall energy of the exercise. It's easy enough for students to be far more focused on the project of designing their contraption than on thinking about inductive reasoning. Two points are worth making in response to this.

First, some of that can be counteracted by making sure that students take seriously the component of the exercise that asks them to present an argument for the likely success or failure of their device. If groups invest themselves in explaining clearly what they think will happen when their device is dropped or employed, they will automatically have to really consider the degree to which past experience informs future predictions.

And second, even if "serious philosophy" is not the main outcome of the exercise, one can still count the activity a success for a number of reasons. Above all, it encourages students to work together on a project that's fun and challenging. But also, by the activity's very nature, students will be engaging in inductive reasoning throughout the length of the activity. They will consistently be making predictions about the future based on past events. So even if this subject is not broached at great length during the course of the exercise, it will sink into students' minds for future exploration. And even though this prediction is based on making such an uncertain prediction, I'm nevertheless confident that it's true.

LESSON PLAN: ASSASSIN GAME

Topic/Question

Epistemology/How is knowledge generated?

Age Group

Fifth grade and up

Time

About thirty minutes

Materials

A space big enough that all students can sit (or stand) in a circle

Description

This is a modification of a well-known summer camp game, alternately known as "Assassin," "Killer," or sometimes "Mafia." It is intended to get students wondering about how knowledge is generated. What are the ways, in other words, by which we come to establish true claims?

To begin, students arrange themselves in a circle, sitting or standing, so everyone can see each other. Explain that they will be playing a game that most of them may be familiar with (having probably played it at summer camp or sleepovers). But in this case, the goal of the game will be slightly different. Instead of merely trying to win, students will reflect on how knowledge—defined broadly as justified true belief—is generated. To do so, a number of different strategies will be explored.

Students are asked to close their eyes. The facilitator then goes around the room and chooses which students will be assassins by tapping them on the shoulder. (Depending on the size of the group, I typically choose one or two assassins.) A good practice is walk around the room talking and occasionally stopping in front of one student or another to create confusion about who is being picked.

Students then are asked to open their eyes. Explain that the class is now in a small town—let's call it Smallville—and living among them are two assassins.[2] The assassins are evil and come out at night to kill unsuspecting citizens. That's what's going to happen tonight.

Next, say that it's been a busy day in Smallville, but now it's time for bed, so everyone goes to sleep—here, students are asked to close their eyes again. At midnight, the assassins awake and, using their nefarious assassin powers, kill one citizen each. By pointing, they indicate the citizen they would like to "kill." Walk over to those students and tap them on the shoulder to indicate that they are dead.

After that's been done, the assassins go back to sleep, and it's now morning in Smallville. The entire class can now see who is dead. (At this point, if they'd like, students who have been assassinated can "die" dramatically. With younger students, this opportunity is usually not passed up. Older students, by contrast, tend to prefer to just "die" quietly.)

The class will now try to figure out who the assassins are, using different methods of trying to generate knowledge. The goal is to see which ones work. Here is a list of the techniques:

- pure hunch
- consensus
- democracy
- monarchy
- bureaucracy
- empirical observation
- rationalistic *a priori* argumentation
- supernatural appeal

Begin with the hunch. A hunch is supposed to be a reason for a belief that has no evidence to support it. Ask students if anyone has a hunch about who the assassin is. Usually someone will say that he or she does. Ask why. If the student refers to something he or she has heard or seen, explain that this isn't a hunch. A hunch isn't supposed to refer to any sort of empirical evidence. Often, this makes it clear to the student that he or she doesn't really have a hunch; it's something else, probably empirical observation, but we will get to that later. So, again ask, "Does anyone have a hunch?"

If someone does, explain that he or she is permitted to rely on that hunch to tell who the assassin is, but if the answer is wrong, he or she will "die." Sometimes this results in students saying that they don't have a hunch after all; other times, a student will want to go with it.

Usually, of course, the hunch does not result in the assassin being identified. But even if it does, this allows students to discuss whether they think hunches are the sort of belief-forming processes that reliably generate knowledge. Students often come up with examples of times they had a hunch about something and it turned out to be true. Again, though, it's worthwhile probing what they mean by a hunch; more often than not, what they call a hunch wasn't really uninformed by some sort of sensory experience. (One of the cleverest responses I've heard was from a seventh grader who said that he had a hunch that hunches were reliable. I asked him why. He said he didn't know; he just had a hunch.)

After this discussion, do another round of the game—students closing their eyes, assassins awaking and killing, the dead being revealed—and then move on to consensus as a technique for generating knowledge. Here "consensus" means that every student has to agree on who the assassin is. Very rarely is consensus achieved, so this technique does not typically generate a guess, much less a correct answer, but again, the attempt leads us into a discussion of whether or not consensus is a reliable belief-forming process that leads to knowledge.

In the occasional instance that consensus is achieved (and it's made extra difficult to do so since even the accused person has to agree), a discussion of something like "group-think" often ensues. I've had a handful of fascinating conversations with students about whether the fact that everyone believes something is a good reason to believe it to be true. Lots of times, students will want to argue that consensus simply is the definition of truth. If everyone believes something, that makes it true, they will assert. This opens the door to pursuing a discussion of whether, say, it was true that the Earth was flat when "everybody" believed it to be. Some students will bite the bullet and say "yes, indeed"; most, however, will be forced to reevaluate their definition of truth as consensus.

The exercise then proceeds through each of the other techniques, with an assassin round between each. (If at some point the assassins are revealed, or if it just seems appropriate, a new game can be started with new assassins in order to get through the list.)

For the democracy technique, have students nominate two candidates for possible assassin, and then vote. (A student who has nominated a candidate dies if that candidate wins the vote but isn't the assassin.)

For the monarchy technique, choose a monarch; he or she has two advisors who advise the monarch as to who the assassin is. The monarch can choose to accept this advice or choose an assassin of his or her own. If the choice is wrong, the monarch does not die; he or she chooses which advisor dies.

For the bureaucracy technique, choose a group of four students who, acting as a kind of city council, have to come to agreement on an assassin candidate and submit it to the larger group for a vote. If their pick is wrong, one of them dies, as voted on by the larger group.

For empirical observation, students offer an argument using evidence gleaned from their senses.

For rationalistic *a priori* argumentation, students have to try to offer an argument that depends on thinking alone. This is pretty tricky; usually students are unable to offer up such an argument, but that's fine, since it allows us to discuss what such an argument would be like. Perhaps an example would be something like this—P1: All assassins are killers. P2: Student X is a killer. P3: Therefore, student X is the assassin.

For supernatural appeal, let one of the students who have already been killed "return from the dead" to offer a suggestion. If the dead student is wrong, then a "living" student who is "possessed" dies.

Other techniques can be added, especially if they are suggested by students. What's philosophically interesting is to have a discussion after each round about the degree to which students think each method is a reliable belief-forming process and whether it was, in fact, effective in identifying the assassin.

To complete the game, it can be illuminating to add one final round. Tell the students to close their eyes, and remind them that if they are tapped on the shoulder, they are assassins. Then go around the room and secretly tap every student on the shoulder. That "night," when the assassins awake, everyone opens his or her eyes ready to "kill," to the general amusement of all. Point out that this is an example of a tautology, a case in which the claim (about the identity of the assassin) is necessarily true. However, as this example illustrates, tautologies are typically not very interesting as articles of knowledge. It is true that a bachelor is always an unmarried male, but the claim "All bachelors are unmarried males" doesn't add a lot of new information to our store of knowledge. It can be effective to end by having students come up with other tautologies. One of my favorites, obviously inspired by the game, was given by a sixth grader: "All assassins are people who kill."

LESSON PLAN: "HYPOTHESIS GENERATION" EXERCISE

Topic/Question

Epistemology/How do we figure things out?

Age Group

Seventh grade and up

Time

About thirty minutes

Materials

Two sets of directions, one for boys and one for girls (see below)

Description

This exercise is designed to do two things: first, and most importantly, it gives students practice in generating and testing hypotheses; second, it allows them to interrogate some of their stereotypical notions of perceived differences between males and females.

The best way to do this exercise is to begin by separating the males and females in the class into two groups on opposite sides of the room. (Groups can also be separated by hair color, age, or even location in the room; however, separating by males and females has proven most effective in getting students to engage fully in the process.) Explain that the class is going to do an activity that will produce data about which students will generate a number of hypotheses and then wonder together about how they might test those hypotheses.

Pass out to both groups papers that appear identical. (In fact, they are slightly different, but don't say so.) The boys' paper includes the diagram shown in the top of figure 3.1, with instructions to memorize this "code." The girls' paper says, "Memorize the following code: Think of the letters as in a tic-tac-toe board." (Their paper includes the picture of the tic-tac-toe board with the letters placed in the proper squares, as illustrated in figure 3.1.)

Give students one minute to commit the code to memory; they will then be shown four words written in the code on the board and will have to translate what is written. They may not work together and may not

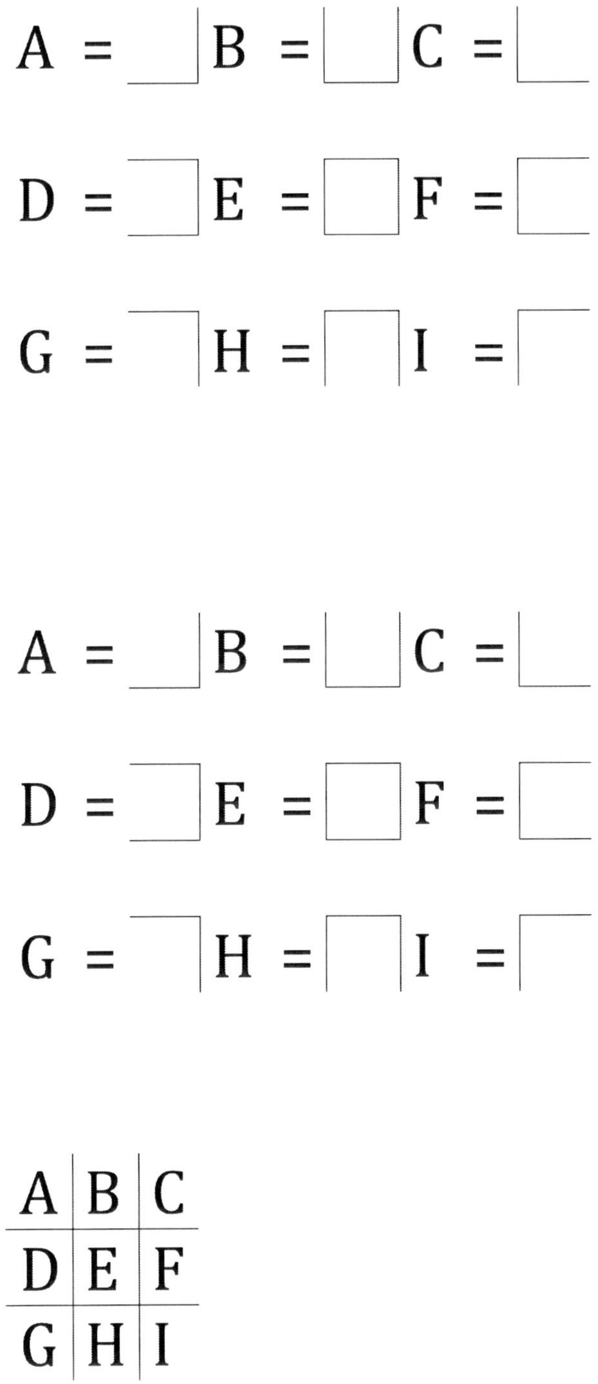

A = ___ B = ___ C = ___

D = ___ E = ___ F = ___

G = ___ H = ___ I = ___

A = ___ B = ___ C = ___

D = ___ E = ___ F = ___

G = ___ H = ___ I = ___

A	B	C
D	E	F
G	H	I

Figure 3.1.

share their answers with anyone else. Absolute quiet is required; anyone caught cheating will be punished. (I don't really punish anyone; I just tell them that to ensure that students don't cheat.)

At the end of one minute, students have to put their papers away and "read" the four words (see figure 3.2). Give them about two minutes to do so, and then reveal the words that the symbols represent.

Ask students to raise their hands depending on how many words each student successfully translated. How many got one right? Two? Three? Four?

Typically, as might be expected, very few boys get even one word correct, while a good number of girls get them all correct.

Ask students to hypothesize why this is so. Every student is to write down at least three hypotheses that explain the discrepancy. Typically, students will offer possibilities like the following:

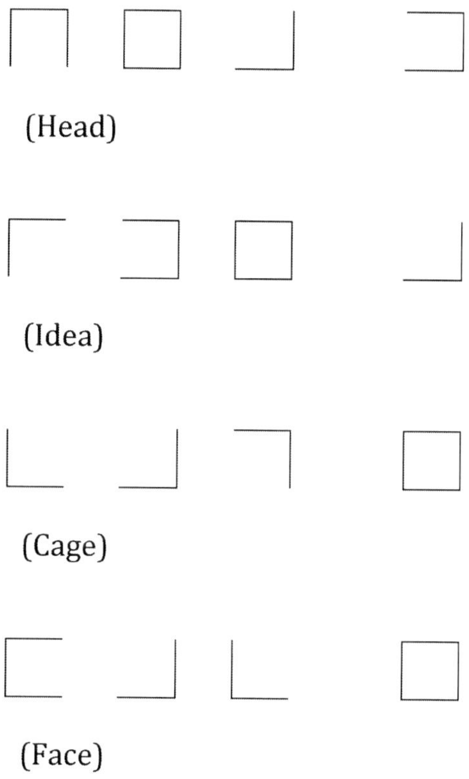

(Head)

(Idea)

(Cage)

(Face)

Figure 3.2.

- Girls are better at spatial memory than boys.
- Girls are smarter than boys.
- Girls are better at concentrating than boys.
- The girls cheated.
- Boys don't take exercises like this seriously.
- Space aliens gave the girls answers by telepathy.

Have a discussion about which two or three hypotheses seem most plausible. Ask students to try to develop a way of testing those hypotheses. Have them write down their possible tests. Talk about them together and then, if possible, attempt the tests.

Eventually, either through the tests or through discussion, it is revealed that the girls had different directions than the boys. This can lead into a fruitful discussion about assumptions and expectations and how they color the conclusions we draw about phenomena we observe.

And, just as an aside, it's interesting to note that often, even after the truth about the different directions has been revealed, many of the girls remain convinced that girls are smarter than boys, and many of the boys remain convinced that the girls cheated.

LESSON PLAN: WHICH STORY IS TRUE?

Topic/Question

Epistemology/How do we ascertain truth?

Age Group

Fifth grade and up

Time

About thirty minutes

Materials

Pieces of paper and pens or pencils for each student to write with

Description

This short exercise is intended to get students wondering about the nature of truth and how we can tell whether something is true or not. It is meant to tease out students' intuitions about what methods we use to determine if a claim is true or false and to help students reflect upon those intuitions both for claims that they make and those that others present to them.

Begin by asking the question "How do we know when a claim is true or false?" Ask students to do a bit of in-class writing in answer to that question and then discuss their answers in the larger group. List on the board the various answers that students give. Typically, they say stuff like "I know a claim is true because it accords with my experience," or "It comes from a reliable source," or "If it's commonplace," or "Whatever most people believe."

It's also interesting to establish criteria for truthfulness. The kinds of responses that typically emerge include "consistency," "reliability," "believability," and "coherence" (although not necessarily expressed in those terms).

Next, tell students that they are going to hear two possible explanations for the same event. They are to assess which one they think is true, and why.

Facilitators can use pretty much any event, as long as they have two different explanations for it. Here's the event I use: I was house-sitting for a friend of mine some years ago at his condo on the beach in San Francisco. When he came home after three weeks away, one of his bedspreads was gone.

Here are the two possible explanations.

First: "I was in his living room one morning, practicing the flute, as I did in those days. The doorbell rang and I went to answer it. Standing in front of me was a naked man. I didn't quite know what to do—and frankly, I didn't know the friend for whom I was house-sitting all that well—so I invited the naked man to come in and sit down. After all, I could see that he was unarmed. He took a seat on the couch and I offered him something to cover up with—the bedspread from the bed in the guestroom just a few feet away. The man just sort of sat there for a while; I went back to practicing my flute while keeping one eye on him.

"Suddenly, he jumped up and said, 'There isn't much time left! There isn't much time left.' He snatched an embroidered pillow that my friend's mom had made for my friend's birthday—and which he had proudly displayed to me as a treasured memento—and, clutching the bedspread around him, ran from the house. I quickly set down my flute and gave chase. The naked man ran across the street to the beach and began pounding down the sand. As I caught up to him, he said again, 'There's no time. It's all about to end.' I thought he might be talking about the day, so I tried to explain that there were still many hours left until sunset, but still, he ran on. At my wits' end about what to do, I grabbed the embroidered pillow from the naked man and then watched as he disappeared down the sand, the bedspread still in his arms. I never saw him or the bedspread again."

Second: "One evening, I was sitting in my friend's living room, drinking beer by the fireplace and listening to records. It was a bit chilly, so I'd grabbed the bedspread from the nearby guestroom bed and had it wrapped around me. Eventually, I got so cold that I stoked up the fire with three or four logs—way more than the little apartment-sized fireplace could really hold. It worked, though; soon I was warm and toasty, and after another beer—my third or so—I guess I dozed off.

"I awoke suddenly to the smell of something burning. Looking down at my feet, I noticed that sparks from the fireplace had ignited the cotton bedspread I had laid over me. In just a few seconds, the entire bottom of the bedspread was on fire and the fire was threatening to spread. I quickly balled up the bedspread and, rushing to the door, threw it outside. There it burst into bigger flames and, in the space of just a minute or so, was almost completely burned up. Fortunately, neither I nor my friend's condo was harmed, but the bedspread was completely ruined. I doused it with some water and put it in the trash."

After relating the event and the two possible explanations for it, ask students, "Which one is the true explanation for what happened, and why do you think so?"

Not surprisingly, the vast majority of students conclude that my second explanation is the true one. Their reasons include statements like "The second one is simply more plausible; naked men don't ring doorbells and no one lets them in the house," "The first explanation has too many extraneous details," "It's obvious that the first explanation is an attempt to get yourself off the hook for something you did," and "I've done something like that second explanation, so it seems believable."

What's surprising, though (and here I often have to do a bit of convincing—as well as remind the students that this happened in the 1970s), is that the first explanation is indeed the true one. That's exactly what happened. Of course, my friend didn't believe me, but that's another story.

This leads into a further discussion of criteria for truth. In the above case, we're working with an odd example because what seemed least plausible was, in fact, true. This can lead to the sharing of other examples of claims whose outlandishness ends up being a point in favor of their being the case.

The next step in the exercise is to ask students to do something similar to what they've just seen their instructor do: write two different explanations for the same event. The class will then try to figure out which explanation is the true one and reflect on this as a way to further inquire into what makes a claim true or false.

Students write their pairs of explanations. Next, divide the class into two groups and have a friendly competition to see if students can figure out which are the true explanations, as well as offer reasons for the explanations they've chosen. The competition is pretty casual, although typically it is scored. What's more important than the outcome of the game is that students have the opportunity to hear various explanations and to assess their plausibility. They can then explore together additional criteria for truth, which positions the class to continue this discussion with other exercises and readings.

One of the most common issues students bring up is whether or not there are any objective criteria for truth. Almost inevitably, someone will claim that there's no such thing as universal truth; it's all subjective. "What's true for me is true for me; what's true for you is true for you" is how it's often put. While many teachers and philosophers bemoan this attitude, it can be very fruitful taking it on, since it indicates that the person arguing for the view has, at least, given some thought to it. So rather than simply rejecting the position out of hand, it can be productive to ask such students what they would say if someone argued that the claim they were making was false. Encourage them to wonder, in other words, whether they are making a claim that purports to be true for not just them but also others. Is there something paradoxical or self-contradictory about their position in other words? This doesn't always move the discussion forward, but it does occasionally have the desired result: as one sixth grader put it, "Stop! You're making my head explode!" If that's not philosophy, I don't know what is.

LESSON PLAN: "WHAT DO I KNOW (ABOUT THIS STRAWBERRY)?" EXERCISE

Topic/Question

Epistemology/What is knowledge?

Age Group

Fifth grade and up

Time

About twenty minutes

Materials

One strawberry (or chocolate square or other candy piece) for each student

Description

The activity is meant to get students wondering about what they know about things in the world and how they know those things. Essentially, it raises questions about what we claim to know via experience and encourages thinking about the relationship between sensory experience and knowledge.

It's a very straightforward activity. Begin by passing out a strawberry (or some other sweet edible) to every student. Ask them to write down everything they know about the strawberry; they are encouraged to use all their senses to generate this knowledge. Students will ask, "Can I eat the strawberry?" Respond with "If it helps you gain knowledge about it, yes." At this point, most do.

After five minutes or so, have students share with each other and the class some of the claims they came up with. Typically, these include statements like those below:

- I know the strawberry is red.
- I know the strawberry has green leaves.
- I know that it smells like strawberry shampoo.
- I know that it tastes sweet and sour.

Naturally, nearly all the claims students make are empirical; almost all the statements they claim to know are derived from sense experience. (Sometimes a student will offer something like "I know the strawberry is a strawberry," which might be construed as an *a priori* claim.) Remind students that it's not uncommon for our senses to deceive us. How many times have they seen a friend across the street, only, upon closer examination, to realize that it's not that person at all? Another possibility is to use some optical illusions to help them notice that what we see is not always what's the case.

Now wonder together whether we really do know the things we think we know.

What works best is to go through the various knowledge claims the students have listed, consider the empirical source of that knowledge, and then wonder whether the claim still counts as knowledge. So, for instance, suppose a student says that he or she knows that the strawberry is a fruit because a teacher told them so. The class would then wonder together whether there have ever been times that our teachers told us something that is false. (Usually, this elicits lots of examples; usually, if the teacher is in the room, he or she gets a kick out of it too.) Given, therefore, that our teachers routinely tell us false things, should it the claim "The strawberry is a fruit" still count as knowledge? Most students will contend that the answer is "yes," but then we can get into a good discussion about how reliable an information source has to be before the alleged knowledge we glean from that source is indeed knowledge. Is 95 percent of the time sufficient? Or 70 percent of the time? What if your source is only correct half the time?

It would be an overstatement to claim that all the discussions that ensue are deeply profound; however, it's usually the case that students do notice that they aren't so certain about some things they previously thought they were certain about. It's relatively easy to build upon that point and explore what it would take for us to really be able to say we know something.

This exercise is often brought to a close by asking students to complete the following fill-in-the-blank "poem": "Something I used to know but I'm not so certain of now is ____."

Here are a few sample responses:

- Something I used to know but I'm not so certain of now is that grownups always know what's right.

- Something I used to know but I'm not so certain of now is that the Seahawks would win the Super Bowl someday.
- Something I used to know but I'm not so certain of now is I could never go to college.

What's heartwarming about such examples is that they show how students are being reflective; in other words, they are thinking about what they think, which is certainly one of the primary goals of doing philosophy.

LESSON PLAN: "CONFIRMATION BIAS" EXERCISE

Topic/Question

Epistemology/When do I know I know something?

Age Group

Sixth grade and up

Time

About twenty minutes

Materials

Pre-printed sheets for students to write on are helpful but not essential

Description

This is an exercise designed to introduce students to the concept of confirmation bias, the tendency we have to find evidence to support claims we already believe. It falls most naturally into an introduction to the scientific method in a critical thinking class, but it can also be effective in pre-college classes to get students thinking and wondering about topics as broad as scientific method and stereotyping. Students tend to come away from this exercise with a pretty good understanding of what confirmation bias is, and we can regularly return to the concept at appropriate points in subsequent classes.

Begin the exercise by handing the students slips of paper printed as shown in figure 3.3. Explain that you have used a rule to generate the sequence that is written down (2, 4, 6). Their challenge is to figure out the rule that's been followed to create the sequence and then to introspect and ask themselves how sure they are that they have identified that rule. They should write down what they think the rule is and a percentage that describes how certain they are, with 100 percent being absolute certainty. If they are 100 percent already (or as certain as they can be), then they should turn their papers over and stop. If they're not certain, they should generate another sequence of numbers to test whether the rule they think is being used actually is the correct rule in order to increase their assurance about that rule. The instructor will come around and check their sequence to see if it fits the rule.

Typically, most students will guess that the rule is "Add 2." And they will say they are around 90 percent sure that this is indeed the correct rule. So, most will do a second sequence, typically something like 8, 10, 12. If you go around and look at what they have written and tell them that yes, indeed, that does fit the rule, most, at this point, will say they are around 95 percent sure (or even higher) and will be satisfied that they have discovered the appropriate rule.

Some, just to be more certain, will try one more sequence, often something like 1, 3, 5 or -8, -6, -4. Both of these sequences fit the rule. Most students rarely try more than three sequences before saying they are as certain as they can be that the rule is "Add 2."

A few students, though, will try to disconfirm their hypothesis, and will try a sequence like 1, 2, 3. Surprisingly, this also fits the rule. They might then try a sequence like 1.1, 1.2, 1.3. This also fits the rule.

The really savvy students will try even harder to disconfirm their hypothesis and will offer a sequence like 6, 4, 2. This doesn't fit the rule. They might then try something like x, x + 1, x + 2. This fits the rule. Typically, a student who has gone this far will correctly identify the rule, which is simply "Increase the sequence," or "Go up."

Sequence	Fits Rule?	Guess Instructor's Rule	How Sure?
2, 4, 6	Y		%
			%
			%
			%
			%
			%

Figure 3.3.

When everyone has said that they are as sure as they can be that they've divined the rule, ask someone who finished in one or two rounds what the rule is. Almost inevitably, the student will say, "Add 2." Confess that this isn't the correct rule. Who has another guess? Eventually, someone will hit on it, and the class can talk about the strategy that student used to figure out what the rule is.

The point to make is that most of us quickly develop the hypothesis that the rule is "Add 2." We then present evidence that confirms what we already believe—hence the sequences like 8, 10, 12. But this doesn't really get us closer to the truth. What we want to do is offer evidence that tries to disconfirm, as opposed to confirming, our hypothesis. So if we imagine that the rule is "Add 2," it's important to try a sequence that would disconfirm that hypothesis, like 1, 2, 3. We might then imagine that the rule is "Increasing integers," but rather than try, say, 4, 5, 6 (which would be evidence that confirms our hypothesis), we should try something like 1.1, 1.2, 1.3, which turns out also to be in accordance with the rule. Our new hypothesis, at this point, might simply be "Increasing numbers," but to attempt to disconfirm that, we might try something that, if true, would force us to revise our hypothesis—hence a sequence like 1, 0, -1. But that sequence does not fit the rule, which is great information to have since it enables us to eliminate possibilities that don't fit.

Without getting too preachy, try to emphasize how valuable it is to find evidence that disconfirms what we already believe, but also how normal it is to only look for—and really only notice—evidence that confirms our preexisting beliefs. As an example of this, you might ask students how many of them think that old people drive too slowly. (Most will agree.) Then get them to reflect upon the last time they saw an old person driving slowly (most have a fairly recent example). When was the last time, by contrast, they saw an old person speeding? Typically, students can't recall such an occasion. That's because they are operating with a confirmation bias. We only notice the slow drivers; the fast ones don't even register since we tend to not even be aware of evidence that conflicts with our preexisting beliefs. That's the source, oftentimes, of stereotypes; once we have, for example, the stereotypical notion that blond people are dumb, then every time we see a blond person saying or doing something dumb, we notice it. We tend not to be aware of blond people saying or doing intelligent things, even if they do.

The point is not that confirmation bias is a bad thing; we need to be able to recognize patterns and draw inferences from them. The danger, though, is that we let the patterns determine the evidence as opposed to drawing upon the evidence to identify the patterns.

To wrap up the exercise, ask students to list five stereotypes they believe to be, in general, true. They should share these with a partner and then each dyad should share with the larger group one stereotype the dyad found interesting. Then open it up to the larger group for evidence that disconfirms this stereotype. One of my favorite examples was the stereotype that school is always boring. A seventh grader—she might have been buttering me up, but so what—said that philosophy class disconfirmed that stereotype.

NOTES

1. Wesley Salmon, "An Encounter with David Hume," edited by Joel Feinberg and Russ Shafer-Landau, *Reason and Responsibility: Readings in Some Basic Problems of Philosophy.*

2. I'm saying "two" for the purposes of this explanation; it could be one or, as I said, sometimes as many as three.

FOUR
What Is Real?

Metaphysics is the area of philosophy that deals with the nature of reality. Obviously, that covers a lot. Questions about what really exists are metaphysical questions. So are questions about the nature of personal identity, such as "What makes me me?" When we wonder about whether we have free will, we are doing metaphysics. And when we explore the nature of time and space, that is also metaphysical inquiry.

The following group of exercises, therefore, ranges pretty broadly. The downside of this is that they may seem somewhat disconnected from one another. The upside, though, is that each can stand alone as its own vehicle of inquiry. Moreover, insofar as students do see connections among the exercises (and in my experience, they often do), their understanding of and appreciation for metaphysic inquiry is enhanced.

LESSON PLAN: REALITY SCAVENGER HUNT

Topic/Question

Metaphysics/What is real?

Age Group

Fifth grade and up

Time

About thirty minutes

Materials

One "Reality Scavenger Hunt" sheet (see below) for each pair of students

Description

This exercise isn't really a scavenger hunt in the traditional sense. Students aren't fanning out across school grounds looking for items like four-leaf clovers, soup cans, and someone wearing a beard. Rather, this scavenger hunt is internal; students work individually, or in pairs, to come up with examples of things that get them wondering about the nature of reality. The exercise works particularly well in conjunction with a reading from Margery Williams's children's classic *The Velveteen Rabbit*, but that's not a prerequisite. In fact, this activity functions well as a stand-alone introduction to wondering about what's real and what isn't. It can be used as an initial foray into metaphysics with students of all ages.

To begin the exercise, ask students to reflect on the question "What is real?" and to wonder how (or even if) they know something is real. Typically, students will say things like they know that school is real because they can't make it end whenever they want. Or they will point out that their desks are real because when they bang on them, they can feel it.

Often, the class will get into some discussion about the difference between reality and dreams. The general consensus is that we know that dreams aren't real because they're so random. Reality isn't like that; it's more stable and predictable. And, as often as not, someone will point out that he or she knows that what's happening in the classroom is real, unlike dreams, because if you pinch yourself, you don't wake up. (And, as often as not, if it's a boy who makes that point, he will illustrate it with a pinch of his own.)

Eventually, it will make sense to segue into the scavenger hunt. This may be a result of the discussion dying down or perhaps making too much of a digression, or it may just be that the students seem hungry for the next thing.

In any case, organize students into pair groups and have them work together to fill out the scavenger hunt sheet below. Encourage them to do their best with each of the categories, but not to stress out if they can't come up with an answer for every single one. While students are working on this task, it's fun to wander around the room and talk with them about some of their answers, but do this somewhat discreetly; you want to discourage pair groups from sharing their responses with other pair groups.

After fifteen or twenty minutes, ask students to wrap up their lists. Break the class into two teams. Give the teams one minute to come up with a name for themselves. Then collect the scavenger hunt sheets, separating them into two stacks—one for each team.

You'll now facilitate a friendly competition between the two teams in which team members will try to identify the proper scavenger hunt category from examples you will read.

Taking a sheet from team A's stack, you will read an example to a member of team B; he or she will answer with the category that example supposedly falls into. So, for example, suppose the pair of students whose list you are looking at has written "vampires" in the category "Something you are glad is not real." You'll read that example aloud and give the student on team B ten or fifteen seconds to answer. If he or she correctly identifies the category, team B will earn a point.

Then take a sheet from team B's stack and repeat the process with a member of team A and so on.

Inevitably, during the game, there will be discussion about whether the examples actually do fit the categories. For instance, one student pair had answered the category "Something that babies think is real but isn't" with "Santa Claus." When I read that aloud, the student I was calling on answered, "Something that is both real and unreal." When I pointed out that his answer was wrong, he argued that Santa Claus is real because we can see him at the mall during the holidays, but unreal because he doesn't actually fly around the world in a sleigh on Christmas Eve delivering toys to all the children in the world. This led the class into an interesting discussion of whether or not a fictional character is real in some sense. We never really got back around to the scavenger hunt, but no one seemed to mind. The discussion became the point, not which team was going to win.

Reality Scavenger Hunt

Come up with examples of each of the following:

- Something that isn't real but appears to be
- Something that is real but appears not to be
- Something that you can't tell if it's real or not
- Something that doesn't matter if it's real or not
- Something that babies think is real but isn't
- Something that babies think is not real but is
- Something that grownups think is real but isn't
- Something that you wish were real
- Something that you are glad is not real
- Something that people in olden times thought was real but now we know isn't
- Something that *has* to be real
- Something that could not possibly be real
- Something that somebody thinks is real but you know isn't
- Something that is both real and unreal
- Something that is neither real nor unreal
- Something that depends on somebody in order to be real
- Something that is real whether anything thinks it is or not

LESSON PLAN: "WHAT MAKES THE TEAM THE TEAM?" EXERCISE

Topic/Question

Metaphysics/What makes something what it is?

Age Group

Fifth grade and up

Time

About fifteen minutes

Materials

Space for students to stand together

Description

This short exercise is a way to get students thinking and wondering about the nature of identity—specifically, what makes something (in this case, a team) what it is. It's a variation on the "Ship of Theseus" thought experiment, only it's done with people instead of planks. The "Ship of Theseus" is a well-known thought experiment in which the boards or planks that make up a boat are slowly, over time, replaced by new boards or planks. Eventually, all the wood in the ship will have been replaced. Meanwhile, in dry dock, a second ship is constructed out of the original boards and planks. The question emerges, then, as to which boat is *really* the ship of Theseus.

The exercise works best if the class has already done other team-style games. Ideally, students will be under the impression that they are being divided into two teams and that those teams will be playing a game that pits them in competition against each other. (This shouldn't be a problem in most cases; I usually present this exercise a few weeks into the quarter; by that time, we've played at least two or three classroom games, and students are used to being assigned groups to work with.)

In any case, the exercise proceeds in this way. Divide the class into two teams, on opposite sides of the room, and tell them that, in a moment, they will begin playing a game. But the first thing that the teams need to do is name their teams and come up with a cheer (as in a cheerleading cheer). Usually, teams have little problem with the first task; typically, they're a little more reticent about the second. It's helpful to model a few cheers for them, explaining that it doesn't have to be any big thing, and that a simple "Go Team, Go!" can suffice. What's important is that everyone on the team knows the cheer and is prepared to demonstrate it. When teams are ready, ask each to tell the team name and present the cheer.

After the teams have done this, say, "We're just about to start the game, but before we do, a few modifications to the membership of each team need to be made." Point out three members of (let's say) team A and tell them to switch places with three members of team B. When they do that, explain that the teams should welcome their new members and then present again their cheers.

After the teams have done that, again say, "We're just about to start, but before we do, we need to do a few more changes in team membership." So again, point out a few more members of each team and ask them to change places. Again, new members are welcomed and the cheer is again presented.

At this point, there usually begins to be some confusion about which team is which and which cheer should be presented. This confusion grows when, right before the start of the "game," the teams are reorganized again. Usually at this point, all but one or two of the original members have switched sides. Again, the team cheers are presented, although there's typically more confusion about which cheer should be done by which team.

Finally, say, "We're really going to start, but one last bit of reorganization is called for." At this point, switch all the remaining original members so that the teams are once again as they were in the beginning, just on different sides of the room.

When the teams are asked to present their cheers now, they're usually unsure of which one to do, or else are quite sure that they should once again present the original cheer. Typically, a good deal of confusion abounds—this is exactly what we want.

It's a puzzle: Which team is where and why? What makes a team the team it is? Is it the cheer? The location of the team in the room? The members? Admit to the class, at this point, that the "game" is the one they've just been engaged in. The point of setting up the teams and rearranging them has been to inspire them to wonder about the source of a team's identity. It's useful to refer to real-world examples here from sports such as when, in football, the Cleveland Browns moved to Baltimore and became the Baltimore Ravens, but then, a few years later, a new Cleveland Browns franchise was created. Which team is really the Browns? Who gets to keep their historical records, for example?

Students usually enjoy this discussion, although some find it frustrating since there's usually some disagreement about what makes a team the team that it is. Try to assure students that this disagreement is to be expected and even celebrated. We can wrangle at some length over the question and, in doing so, develop a clearer sense in our own minds about the nature of identity not just for teams, but for individuals as well.

Draw this exercise to a close by having students do some writing about what they learned from it, as well as any additional questions they still have. Ask them to complete the following sentence for a fill-in-the-blank "poem": "What best defines my team is its _____."

After students have done this, go around the room, sharing answers. Often the answers have a somewhat circular quality, as in "What best defines my team is its team spirit," or even "What best defines my team is the team." This can occasionally lead to more speculation on identity and other related metaphysical questions, and it has, in other instances, led to further exploration of the qualities of various teams in different sports—perhaps not as "philosophical" a topic, but one that can nevertheless be interesting and fruitful.

LESSON PLAN: WHAT MAKES ME ME?

Topic/Question

Metaphysics/Who or what am I?

Age Group

Sixth grade and up

Time

About an hour

Materials

Pieces of paper and pens or pencils for each student to write with, index cards, and the Calling Cards Tournament Bracket (see below)

Description

The point of this exercise is to explore the question "What makes me me?" It is intended to inspire students to wonder about what their essential characteristics are. The hope is that participants come away from the activity with a better sense of the fundamental properties or qualities that uniquely distinguish them—and each of us—from someone else.

To begin the exercise, have students write down on a sheet of paper ten qualities that describe them. As an example, I offer this list of my own. I'm a

- father
- husband
- community college teacher
- bicycle commuter
- vegetarian
- Pittsburgh Steelers fan
- right-hander
- male
- dog owner
- Macintosh computer user

Students then set about to create their own lists. When they've all managed to do so (or come reasonably close), have students pair up and share their lists; they are urged to use this input from their classmates to modify or add to their groups of ten.

Then ask if any students would like to volunteer their lists for the larger group. One of these volunteers will then take part in a shared example during the next part of the exercise.

For that next part, ask students to think a bit about essences and what it is about a property that would make us consider it an essential property of something. Typically, without too much prodding, they can arrive at some sort of agreement that one thing about essential properties is that they tend to be those that are long-lasting and persist over time. Qualities that come and go, that change with the seasons, seem to be less essential. So, we can examine our lists of personal properties with that criterion in mind.

Ask students to look at their lists and cross out any of the qualities that weren't true about them a year ago; presumably, a quality like this, that has emerged only in the last year, wouldn't count as essential. (This isn't always the case, and can lead to some interesting discussion, but the basic point tends to be fairly uncontentious, and certainly in keeping with how essential properties have typically been conceived of.)

Discuss this; then ask students to cross out any qualities that weren't true about them two years ago. More discussion ensues; then ask them to cross out any qualities that weren't true about them five years ago. Next, they are asked to cross out any qualities that weren't true about them when they were ten years old. Then five years old. And then, finally, they are asked to cross out any properties that weren't true about them when they were a year old.

Looking at my list above illustrates a puzzle, which we then discuss. What's left, in my case, is really only one quality: male. (Right-hander might count, too; there's room for discussion about qualities like this and whether, for instance, right-handedness is a quality we possess from birth. This can be interesting and fruitful, but it's slightly beside the point.) The puzzle, therefore, is this: We've agreed that our essential qualities—those that make us who we are—are those that last, but when we winnow down our lists to those qualities that have persisted in our own lives for the longest time, we are left with only the very most generic qualities. So, for example, while maleness may indeed be an essential quality of David Shapiro, it does nothing, really, to pick me out uniquely.

Move, then, into the second part of this exercise, which is to think more carefully about what makes us who we are. To explore this question, hand out to students a list of what we might consider the essential characteristics of a person, arranged in a kind of tournament bracket so they can be paired off against each other (see figure 4.1).

These characteristics represent very broad, but easily understandable, ways of acting or behaving that students can recognize as either describing them or not. For instance, some of the characteristic "essences" are "building things," "designing things," "getting to the heart of matters," and "getting things right."

Students then take about twenty minutes to complete their "tournament brackets." Urge them, as they work, to not "overthink" the essence descriptions. They are purposely somewhat vague and ambiguous; the idea is to read each pair and pretty much go with one's gut reaction as to which descriptor is a better fit. If students think that both descriptors are apt, they can move both into the next "round" on the sheet; similarly, if neither seems appropriate, neither must be moved forward. What students do have to note, though, is that there will come a time as they get to the end of the "tournament" when some hard choices will have to be made. Eventually, they will get down to just three descriptors, from which they must then choose the one they think best fits them.

When students have chosen their "essence," they are then asked to write it down on one side of an index card; on the other side, they are to write a paragraph about why they chose that as their essence and how, in their everyday lives, they manifest this essence in their behavior.

We then have a discussion in which is introduced the well-known thought experiment that involves our minds switching place with our bodies. One well-known representation of this has two people—it works well to have it be the instructor and a student—both working as electrical workers on high-voltage wires. Because a severe electric shock can result in a loss of memory, every day, when we report to work, we upload the entire contents of our minds onto computer hard disks so that, should we suffer an electric shock, we will be able to download our minds back into our bodies, thus losing only that one day's memories.

Well, sure enough, one day we both receive terrible electric shocks. We're rushed to the mental uploading facility, but because the technician isn't paying attention, he uploads the student's mind into my body and vice versa. We awaken, look at our bodies, and wonder, "Who am I?"

Questions to pose at this point are "Whose house does my body go home to? And why?" A relatively rich discussion usually follows, with students considering both possibilities: that my body with the student's mind goes to my house or that my mind in the student's body does. The puzzles inherent in both these possibilities give rise to the next part of the exercise, which is to have students "simulate" the mind/body switch.

Have them hand in all the index cards on which they've written their essences and the descriptions thereof. Shuffle the cards up and hand them back, making sure that no student gets his or her own card. Students are then asked to imagine that this new essence has been placed in their bodies.

Students then have a few minutes to familiarize themselves with their new essence and to really take seriously the idea that this personality is now in their body, replacing the personality they had before.

For the next part of the exercise, students are asked to move about the room and mingle, doing their best to relate to each other from the perspective of their new identity. During this activity, their goal is to express themselves in this new way but also, if possible, to try to find their original personality. (This always tends to be a little bit confusing; some students find it incredibly difficult and frustrating. But overall, it's fun and worthwhile, and it only lasts about five minutes.)

At the conclusion of this part of the exercise, debrief and discuss. Ask students what worked and what didn't, what was difficult and what

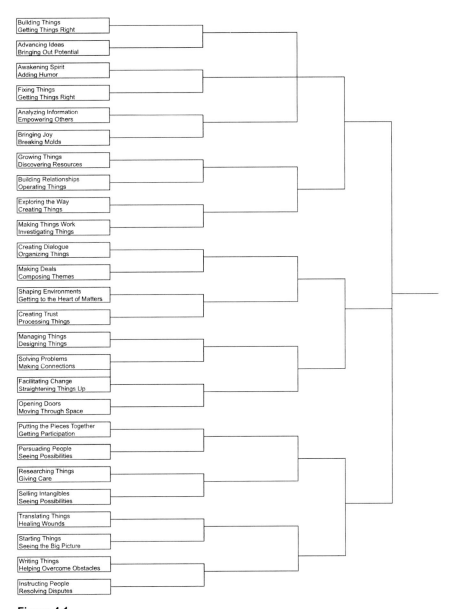

Figure 4.1.

seemed easier. Encourage them to take on the question "Who were you with the new essence in your body?" And wonder together whether this "simulation" provided any insight into the questions raised by the earlier thought experiment.

It's fascinating to see how students respond. Middle school students, in particular, find the essence-switching exercise very challenging. I believe this is because they are just coming into an understanding of who they are; thus, it's especially difficult for them to adopt the essence of someone else. "I'm a person who 'brings humor,'" a boy will say. "I can't possibly manage to 'heal things.' That's just weird!"

But even older students struggle with the switch. When I do this exercise in college classes, I inevitably hear from participants who find themselves unable to imagine what it would be like to be different than they are. Of course, this opens the door to exactly the sort of philosophical point we want to ponder together: What makes a person the person he or she is? If it turns out to be this essence (or something like that) after all, then why do we relate to each other as bodies? How could we tell if someone was telling the truth to us about being "trapped" in another person's body? And why (as we talked about for a long time in a high school class) do we spend so much time and energy worrying about how we look to others? If we are really our essences, why would that matter?

Finally, as a "capstone" to this exercise, ask students to collectively write a fill-in-the-blank "poem." Each student is asked to write down his or her completion of the following sentence: "I'm the only person I know who _____."

When they have done this, go around the room, and (with the pass rule in effect) let each student offer his or her example. Some memorable ones include "I'm the only person I know who has six toes," "I'm the only person I know who likes calculus," "I'm the only person I know who has two moms," and "I'm the only person I know who has had a near-death experience."

Not only can this sharing opportunity be both funny and poignant, but it also brings us back to the original question about what makes us who we are, and it does so in a way that students find intriguing, accessible, and pertinent to their everyday lives.

LESSON PLAN: COULD ANYTHING ELSE HAVE HAPPENED?

Topic/Question

Metaphysics/Do we have free will?

Age Group

Fifth grade and up

Time

About twenty minutes

Materials

Room for students to move around and a big bag of dominoes

Description

This is a brief activity designed to get students wondering about the so-called Problem of Free Will. It doesn't purport to offer a solution; it just attempts to raise the question of how human beings can be said to make free choices in a deterministic universe, one that behaves according to fundamental natural laws.

Begin the exercise by offering students a choice and telling them that it's possible to predict, with some certainty, what their answers will be. Before they are given the choice, write down on a piece of paper that students can't see the following phrase: "Get out of class five minutes early."

Then offer students the choice: Would they like to write a ten-page paper or would they like to get out of class five minutes early? Ask them to write down their answers on a piece of paper. Then say that you have already written down what can be predicted that all of them, or nearly all of them, have written. Hold up the piece of paper.

Usually, students are not too impressed; they will say things like "Well, of course we chose to get out of class five minutes early over writing a ten-page paper; it's no big deal that you could predict that."

The reasonable response is to agree; it *is* no big deal. But doesn't the fact that a person could predict how they would answer a data point raise a question about whether their choices really are free? Some students agree; others remain skeptical.

Ask them to try another test, this one a bit more involved. Admit that some students may be familiar with the example about to be shared; if so, appeal to them not to let on to their classmates but simply to take the example seriously and keep their mouths shut.

The example goes like this: Ask students to write down a number between 1 and 9. Then take that number and multiply it by 9. Now, take that number and add its digits together to make a single number. Now, subtract 5 from that number to get a new number. Now, count forward in the alphabet that many numbers. Now, think of a country that begins with that letter of the alphabet. Now, take the second letter of that country's name and think of the name of an animal that begins with that letter. Now, think of a color that animal comes in.

Here, pause a moment and write something down on a piece of paper. Hold up that paper and say, "This is what you are thinking of: a gray elephant from the *e* in Denmark."

On average, well over than half of the students will admit that that's exactly what they were thinking of and will be impressed that it could be predicted after so many steps. How many of them now wonder whether their choices are actually made freely?

An interesting discussion usually ensues, even though many students will see the "trick." (Any number times 9 equals a number whose digits, when added together, total 9; when you subtract 5 from that, you get 4; the most familiar country name beginning with the letter *d* is "Denmark"; the most common animal name beginning with the letter *e* is "elephant"; elephants are usually gray.) Also, some students, especially ones who are familiar with the puzzle, will try to derail it by answering something like "A brown jackal from the *j* in Djibouti" or "An orange orangutan from the *o* in Dominican Republic."

For the unconvinced, offer one more exercise. Get students to pair up, and begin a "Rock, Paper, Scissors," or Rochambeau, tournament. Best two out of three wins; victors go to the front of the room.

Play through the tournament until there are only two remaining; they play a best-three-out-of-five final, and the champion is crowned.

Now ask whether it was inevitable that the person who won would win. Typically, students take dissenting positions, but predominantly, most will argue that it wasn't inevitable at all. How, though, they wonder together, could that have taken place? After all, if we trace back the cause-and-effect relationships from the beginning of the tournament, there's only one way things could have happened—the way they actually did. So, there's a puzzle here, which we can exploit in conversation. And if we think of the choices we make in our own lives, it's like that too; given the choices we've made, how could anything have come out differently?

After pursuing this line of conversation a while, wonder aloud whether, if the class were to play the tournament again, it would come out the same way; then do it. Almost always, someone else wins. (In fifteen years of my playing this game with students, only once did the same student win both rounds.)

How does this result square with the notion of free will? Pursue this line of questioning for a while, not pressing for any particular answer—just see where the discussion takes you.

At this point, it's fun to illustrate the so-called hard determinist answer to the problem of free will by having students create a domino chain. (The hard determinist view is the view that we live in an entirely cause-and-effect universe, that all effects are determined by previous causes or states of affairs, and that, essentially, free will is an illusion.) I give groups of three or four students two minutes to see how long a chain they can create. When the time is up, one of them knocks down the first domino in the chain, and the others fall in sequence; we use this as a model for the hard determinist position.

Next, briefly introduce the other two main perspectives on the problem of free will: the so-called indeterminist and compatibilist positions. Indeterminism is the view that everything in the universe happens randomly, and that cause-and-effect is an illusion. Compatibilism, also known as "soft determinism," is the view that even though the universe is deterministic, some conception of free will is, at least, compatible with that. We want to be able to distinguish between choices that are truly out of our control and those that we do have some free choice in making. The paradigmatic example is to contrast a case in which a robber holds a gun to your head and demands that you give him your wallet or he will shoot you with a case in which the same person merely asks you to give him your wallet. While, at some level, you do have a "choice" not to give him your wallet, in the first case it's clear that your decision to do so was forced in a way that it wasn't in the second case.

Pass out dominoes to groups of students and ask them to illustrate these positions using the dominoes. For instance, students might illustrate compatibilism by creating a line of dominoes that falls one after another but can be stopped or changed mid-course. Or they might illustrate indeterminism by setting up dominoes all over the place and knocking them down randomly.

Once students have created and demonstrated their models, wrap up the lesson by coming back again to wondering about whether we really are free. Ask students to complete a fill-in-the-blank "poem" with the phrase "One thing in my life I wish I could have done differently was _____."

Students share their responses, and we end up by wondering together whether we really could have done that thing differently. Some students argue that they could have; others say they really had no choice. The dissent is good because it helps illustrate how "live" the debate over the problem of free will remains, both for laypeople and professional philosophers alike.

LESSON PLAN: GOT A MINUTE?

Topic/Question

Metaphysics/What is time?

Age Group

Sixth grade and up

Time

About thirty to forty minutes, depending on the size of the class

Materials

A stopwatch or watch with a second hand

Description

This exercise is meant to do two things: first, it raises questions about the nature of time—in particular, our subjective experience of it; second, it provides a classroom forum that encourages every student's voice to be heard.

The activity begins with a simple question: "What is time?" The intent is to tease out students' intuitions about time. Is it a thing? Is it merely a convention? Did it exist before human beings? Will it still be here after we're gone? Usually, this will get students pondering and talking about the difference between the measurement system (seconds, minutes, hours, and so on) and what is being measured, although many students will contend that time is entirely conventional; they will maintain that before the measurement system was invented, time didn't exist. This gives rise to a puzzle, however: How did anything change or evolve? When presented with this, many students will incline toward a view that time is something like change. With this in mind, we can proceed to the first activity in the lesson, which is really a "non-activity."

If time is somehow connected to change, we wonder, then does time stop when nothing changes, or at least slow down when things change less?

Ask students to stand up and prepare to walk around the room for thirty seconds. They are to walk relatively quickly, but to do so in a cautious, aware state, making sure they don't bump into each other. On the count of three, set them off, and time them for thirty seconds, after which they are to stop and return to their seats.

Now, ask them to prepare to sit quietly, doing their best not to move a muscle or say a word. On the count of three, they start doing so; again, time them for thirty seconds.

How did the length of time of these two events differ, if at all? Was one thirty-second period "faster" than the other? Typically, most students say that silent sitting took longer. So did time actually speed up and slow down, or did it just feel that way? Opinions tend to differ on this, so we'll try something similar to explore the question in greater depth.

Ask students to stand up and close their eyes. Tell them that they are going to be timed for fifteen seconds, and ask them to raise their hands when they think fifteen seconds has passed. Time them, and note how close most students are to hitting the mark, as compared to those who raise their hands early or late.

Now, ask them to raise one leg in the air as high as they can, close their eyes (they can hold on to their desks or chairs for balance), and, once again, put their hands in the air when fifteen seconds has passed.

Not surprisingly, most students raise their hands earlier the second time. Fifteen seconds seems a lot longer when you're exerting yourself. Again, we wonder whether time really did slow down or if it merely felt like it. Here, in my experience, students often seem a bit more puzzled. Given that so many people experience the latter period as longer, maybe time really did slow down. In any case, suppose everyone in the world simultaneously experienced time as moving more slowly. Wouldn't it then make sense to say that, as a matter of fact, it was?

At this point, there is often a lot of simultaneous talking; everyone wants to speak, so no one can get a word in edgewise. What we need to do, therefore, is give everyone their own time to speak. Explain that, presently, everyone will have the chance to "have the floor" by themselves, with no interruptions. Each student is to craft a one-minute-long "rant" on any subject they choose. It can be about what you've been discussing, but it doesn't have to be. However, the rant will be delivered in pieces—first thirty seconds, then fifteen, then ten, then five, and then, as a bonus, one second.

Give students three to five minutes to write their rant. Then arrange to present. Ideally, students sit in a circle, but it can work almost as well by having them stand and deliver their rants one after another.

Keep time as each student talks, and cut them off at exactly thirty seconds. Then go through a second time (starting with the student who went last the first time), with each student having just fifteen seconds. Then again, with ten; then with five. The bonus round, in which each student has just one second, is sort of silly, but can be great fun, as each class member has about enough time to say just a word or two.

Afterward, talk about perceptions of time during the exercise. Many times students are shocked at how long thirty seconds of ranting time is. (Oddly enough, students who tend, as a general rule, to dominate discussions often have the most difficulty filling thirty seconds of time.)

Finally, return to the question, "What is time?" And to end the lesson, it works well to do a fill-in-the-blank "poem." Ask students to think about what they would do if they had a minute to do anything they wanted. The fill-in-the-blank, then, is this: "If I had a minute to do anything I wanted, I would _____."

Here are a few sample responses from a group of sixth graders:

- If I had a minute to do anything I wanted, I would go skiing.
- If I had a minute to do anything I wanted, I would sneak into the movies.
- If I had a minute to do anything I wanted, I would spy on my brother.
- If I had a minute to do anything I wanted, I would see my grandma who died last year.
- If I had a minute to do anything I wanted, I would pitch for the Mariners.
- If I had a minute to do anything I wanted, I would fly.

FIVE

What Is Art?

Some of the most provocative and effective thought experiments related to the philosophy of art can be found in the excellent book *Puzzles about Art: An Aesthetics Casebook* by Margaret Battin, John Fisher, Ron Moore, and Anita Silvers. I regularly use a number of the case studies in the collection to motivate discussion on questions like "What is art?" "What is beauty?" and "Can art be immoral?" In fact, one of the exercises in this section, "Smoke," comes pretty much directly from the book.

Additionally, however, it's illuminating to get students doing some art when they talk about aesthetics. The "Blind Painter" exercise from chapter 1 is one way to do that in a manner that's pretty nonthreatening even for students who tend to be somewhat art-averse.

The "Art Market" exercise in this chapter also gives students a chance to do some drawing. Teachers interested in exploring aesthetics with their students should also look for other opportunities to get kids involved in art-making; probably the best way to motivate discussions about the nature of art is to inspire the practice of doing it. And as I always counsel students, especially in higher grades, "Never pass up an opportunity to use crayons."

LESSON PLAN: AESTHETICS SCAVENGER HUNT

Topic/Question

Aesthetics/What is art?

Age Group

Fifth grade and up

Time

About thirty minutes

Materials

One "Aesthetics Scavenger Hunt" sheet (see next page) for each pair of students

Description

Unlike the "Reality Scavenger Hunt" in chapter 4, this exercise requires students to make an external search for the items in question. Ideally, this would be done on a field trip to a local museum, but it can also be done by having students look through art books or, more typically, search museum websites on the Internet.

The activity doesn't really require much in the way of "tee-up," although usually it's preceded by some discussion about the nature of art, using one or more of the thought experiments in *Puzzles about Art*.

As with the "Reality Scavenger Hunt," it works best to have students pair up for their exploration. Again, encourage them to do their best with each of the categories, but not to worry too much if they can't come up with an answer for every single one.

Depending on whether the activity is taking place in a museum, with books, or virtually, students will need more or less time to complete their sheets. In a museum, an hour is probably about right; with books or online, maybe half that.

Aesthetics Scavenger Hunt

- Find an example of an artwork that challenges your definition of what art is. Do you think this piece is *really* art? Why or why not?
- Find an example of a work of art that could have been done by a chimpanzee. If it *had* been done by a chimpanzee, would it still be art? Why or why not?
- Find an example of an artwork you think is beautiful. Why do you think it's beautiful? What standards of beauty does it reveal?
- Find an example of an artwork you think is ugly. Why do you think it's ugly? What standards of ugliness does it reveal?
- Find an example of an artwork that is so ugly that it's beautiful. Or find one that is so beautiful that it's ugly. Say why you judge it the way you do. Or explain why no such work of art is possible.
- Find an example of a piece of art that teaches you something. What does it teach you and why?
- If you were in an art museum and there was a fire and you could only save one piece of art, which would it be? Why? Suppose that you could either save that piece of art *or* a museum guard. Which would you save? Why? Suppose it was a choice between the piece of art and a cat that lived in the museum. Which one would you save? Why?
- What piece of art do you find the most emotionally or intellectually troubling? Would you be in favor of banning that artwork from public view? Why or why not?
- Find out which work of art in a museum is worth the most money (or at least is one of the most valuable). Do you think that this is the best piece of art in the museum? Why or why not?
- If you were a piece of art, which piece would you be? Why?

In any case, once students have completed their sheets, discussion follows. It usually works fine to simply turn things over to the students and ask them which of the scavenger hunt items they'd most like to talk about. But if this doesn't seem to get things rolling, a teacher might also collect the scavenger hunt sheets and randomly choose from the items to motive dialogue. A third technique that has worked sometimes is to have pair groups trade their papers with other pair groups and compare their answers. This leads to lively conversations among parties of four, but doesn't necessarily get the whole class involved simultaneously.

LESSON PLAN: "SMOKE"

Topic/Question

Aesthetics/Is art purely subjective?

Age Group

Sixth grade and up

Time

About twenty minutes

Materials

A blackboard or whiteboard

Description

This exercise comes from *Puzzles about Art*. It's an excellent "tee-up" to issues related to aesthetics because it does such a fine job of inspiring students to wonder about the nature of aesthetics claims. In particular, the exercise helps raise questions about how subjective (or objective) we take art to be. Most students, pre-philosophically, will contend that art is completely subjective. "If you think it's art, then it's art" will be their general attitude. "Smoke," however, provides an experience that calls that into question to some degree. Students may come out of the exercise as firmly convinced as ever that art is completely subjective; however, they will have taken part in an activity that enabled them to interrogate that view.

The exercise itself is deceptively simple. Basically, it's an animal-vege-table-mineral-type game in which a group of players try to guess the identity of a famous individual by asking questions of a single player who knows the answer. The wrinkle is that the players can only ask metaphorical questions of the form "If this person were a _____, what type of _____ would they be?" (The reason the game is called "Smoke" is because the paradigmatic question is "If this person were smoke, what type of smoke would they be?")

After explaining the rules of the game, think of a famous person and give the class one broad hint about that individual in terms of what arena he or she occupies (e.g., film star, politician, athlete). Then the game begins.

Go around the room; each student gets to ask one question. Usually students have no trouble grasping the concept; they tend to ask questions like "If this person were a car, what type of car would they be?" or "If this person were a film, what type of film would they be?" Sometimes they try to push the rules a little and want to ask questions like "If this person were a gender, what gender would they be?" or "If this person were in a famous movie, what movie would that be?" If this happens, gently inform the student that this is an illegitimate question and give them the chance to ask another.

As you answer, write each answer on the board, so they can be reviewed when the game is over. After all the students have asked their questions, ask them to write down on a small scrap of paper who they think the person is. Then collect the scraps and go through them to see if anyone has correctly identified the person. If so, write the famous person's name, along with two other names, on the board so students can vote on who the class thinks the person is. (If no one has correctly identified the person, just pretend that there was one right answer and put that name up along with two others.)

Vote on the person, discuss that choice, and then reveal the right answer. At this point, the philosophically interesting part of the activity begins because now the class can review answers given to the "smoke" questions that were asked and assess them. Students routinely will take exception to one or more of the metaphors that emerged, arguing that so-and-so is not like that such-and-such at all. For instance, one time the person in question was the actor Johnny Depp, and I'd answered the question "If this person were a car, what type of car would they be?" with "Rolls-Royce." Students, almost universally, were adamant that Johnny

Depp would never be such a staid, old brand; rather, they argued, he would be something flashy and fast like a Maserati or a Ferrari.

At this point, it can be pointed out that here they are applying objective (or at least quasi-objective) standards to something that, initially, they all said was purely subjective. How can they judge my artistic choices to be mistaken? And if they can, how broadly does this pertain to other artistic perspectives?

Usually, a pretty rich discussion ensues. Again, as mentioned earlier, this doesn't necessarily convince (nor is it my aim to convince) students that art is not entirely subjective; it does, however, get them wondering about the question in ways that they typically haven't before. And this sets the stage for further discussion of aesthetics and the philosophy of art, both in the classroom and beyond it.

LESSON PLAN: ART MARKET

Topic/Question

Aesthetics/What makes art valuable?

Age Group

Sixth grade and up

Time

About forty-five minutes

Materials

Blank paper and crayons or colored pencils for each student to draw with, a list of "artist types" (described below), and enough play money to give each student about $250,000

Description

The intent of this exercise is to get students wondering about the nature of value in art. It also raises questions about the relationship between artistic appreciation and commercialism, essentially providing a forum to explore the degree to which someone's affection for a piece of art translates into its monetary worth. Finally, it stimulates discussion about what factors figure into our assessment of a work of art's quality, and the degree to which our perception of that quality is influenced by what we know about the creator of that work.

To begin the exercise, students are given a blank sheet of paper and a set of drawing materials; crayons or colored pencils are ideal. Each student is then given an artistic identity; I hand out small slips of paper with a different type of artist on each. Students are told not to tell anyone else what type of artist they are.

Here is the list of artist types. Depending on the size of the class, there will be some duplicates, but that's okay.

- amateur artist
- art student
- conceptual artist
- child artist
- first-time artist
- locally famous artist
- movie-star artist
- nationally famous artist
- New York City gallery artist
- production-line artist
- professor of art
- rock-star artist
- world-famous dead artist
- world-famous living artist

Give students about twenty minutes to create a work of art in the style of the artist type they have been assigned. Students can make anything they want; they should just do their best to make a work that reflects that artist's style. Often, they have questions about this; just tell them to have fun and do the best they can—this is generally sufficient. Very occasionally a student will get completely stuck; when this happens, simply let the student draw whatever he or she likes, without worrying about the artist type.

When students are done with their pictures, they are to write, in very small letters on the back of their artwork, the type of artist they are; this is so the facilitator can read it but no one else can.

The works of art are then posted on the wall and the class has a short "art opening" where they mingle and look at the different works; no one is allowed to say which piece is theirs, though, and no one should try to figure out what type of artist has done the piece.

Next, pass out "money" to the students. Every student gets pre-printed rectangles of paper in various denominations: $100, $500, $1,000, $10,000, and $100,000, totaling $258,000 (5 x $100, 5 x $500, 5 x $1,000, 5 x $10,000, and 2 x $100,000). (These are just suggested amounts; all that really matters is that students each get the same amount.)

The facilitator then "auctions" off the pieces one by one. It's a good idea not to start with the world-famous artist, but other than that, things can proceed fairly randomly. It's fun to pretend to be an auctioneer at Sotheby's and say a few words about the piece and then open the bidding. Students can bid on any piece, even their own, as long as they have enough money. When the artwork sells, give the money to the student who has made the artwork; he or she then has that money to spend on other works. The goal of the auction is to acquire artwork that appeals to you but also to maximize the value of your art collection.

As each piece is sold, reveal what type of artist has done the work and the market value of such a type of artwork, as follows:

- amateur artist: $200
- art student: $300
- conceptual artist: $1,500
- child artist: $0
- first-time artist: $100
- locally famous artist: $10,000
- movie-star artist: $15,000
- nationally famous artist: $150,000
- New York City gallery artist: $75,000
- production-line artist: $250
- professor of art: $3,000
- rock-star artist: $25,000
- world-famous dead artist: $40 million
- world-famous living artist: $3 million

After all the pieces are sold—and often during the auction—students reflect on the relative value of the pieces. There are usually some pieces that are more desirable than others; there have been times when very creative works of art have been made. Typically, students want these, whether they are done by "world-famous" artists or not. It's odd, then, that we will have a situation where such a work ends up going for a very high price, only for the bidders and buyer to discover that it was done by, say, a "child artist" and has no market value.

Usually, a good deal of competitive spirit emerges during the auction. Students want to maximize the value of their collections. Sometimes a group will create a consortium in which they pool their funds to acquire what they think are the most valuable pieces. This should be encouraged, as it can also lead to interesting discussions about artistic value and what collectors are trying to do—whether they are interested in acquiring pieces they love or pieces that have value.

Finish up the activity by having students write about what possessions they have that they consider most valuable and why. To get this off the ground, ask them to imagine that their house is on fire and they can only save three things from destruction. (This being a philosophical thought experiment, the particulars of size or weight don't matter. I do, however, draw the line at saving what one creative fifth grader proposed: his house!)

Sometimes we also use this as an opportunity to explore a thought experiment from *Puzzles about Art* in which you are faced with saving either the *Mona Lisa* or the guard who stands next to it from a fire in the Louvre. Again, what emerges from this can be a rich conversation about value, not just in art, but in all aspects of our experience.

SIX
What Is the Right Thing to Do?

Ethics is the subfield of philosophy that explores the nature of right and wrong. For most students, this is not only the most familiar branch of philosophical inquiry but also the most compelling. From a very young age, children are naturally intrigued by questions about what a person ought to do and why. And by the time kids reach middle school, issues of fairness and equity occupy much of their classroom behavior and discussion.

Consequently, it's relatively easy to motivate philosophical discussion about ethics; for many students, doing philosophy *is* doing ethics.

The following group of exercises explores a number of topics that fall under the subfield of ethics; some investigate more theoretical issues, like the role of principles in moral reasoning, while others take on more applied-ethics topics, like animal rights. All, though, have been successful in inspiring ethical inquiry; most of the time, they've also been fun for students and teacher alike.

LESSON PLAN: "RING OF GYGES" DIARY

Topic/Question

Ethics/Why should I be moral?

Age Group

Sixth grade and up

Time

About twenty minutes

Materials

"Ring of Gyges" story from Plato's *Republic*

Description

This is a relatively short exercise intended to get students thinking about ethics, particularly the question "Why should I be moral?"

Begin by wondering together in a general way about right and wrong. Gently ask students to share something they've done in their lives that they believe was wrong. (To prime the pump for this, I'll usually give them an example from my own life; typically, I'll tell them about the time I was eight years old and I lied to my mom about stealing matches so I could go in the woods with my friends and light them.)

Generally, students aren't shy about providing examples; in fact, it's usually more of a challenge to get them to move on from telling me stories about how they were mean to their siblings or cheated on tests or took something that wasn't theirs than it is to get them started. Nevertheless, eventually transition to a second question: "Can you give me examples of times when you wanted to do something wrong but didn't?" (Here, I'll offer an example like the time—only yesterday, let's say—when I was in the supermarket and could have stolen the expensive cheese I wanted but didn't.)

After hearing their examples, ask what it was that prevented them from doing the bad thing that they wanted to do: "Why didn't you do it? How come you stopped yourself?"

Usually, most students will respond that they were afraid they would get caught. (Some might offer other possibilities, such as that they really think stealing is wrong or that they wouldn't want to be treated poorly themselves, but in general, the threat of punishment is the prevailing answer.)

It's easy, therefore, to segue into the question that lies at the root of the "Ring of Gyges" story: "What if you wouldn't get caught? Suppose you could get away with whatever you wanted; what would you do then?"

At this point, read or paraphrase the "Ring of Gyges" story. Here's one translation of it:

According to the tradition, Gyges was a shepherd in the service of the king of Lydia; there was a great storm, and an earthquake made an opening in the earth at the place where he was feeding his flock. Amazed at the sight, he descended into the opening, where, among other marvels, he beheld a hollow brazen horse, having doors, at which he stooping and looking in saw a dead body of stature, as appeared to him, more than human, and having nothing on but a gold ring; this he took from the finger of the dead and re-ascended. Now the shepherds met together, according to custom, that they might send their monthly report about the flocks to the king; into their assembly he came having the ring on his finger, and as he was sitting among them he chanced to turn the collet [decorative front] of the ring inside his hand, when instantly he became invisible to the rest of the company and they began to speak of him as if he were no longer present. He was astonished at this, and again touching the ring he turned the collet outwards and reappeared; he made several trials of the ring, and always with the same result—when he turned the collet inwards he became invisible, when outwards he reappeared. Whereupon he contrived to be chosen one of the messengers who were sent to the court; where as soon as he arrived he seduced the queen, and with her help conspired against the king and slew him, and took the kingdom.[1]

Talk about the story a bit (usually students have questions about how the ring works and if, like the Ring of Power in *Lord of the Rings*, it would eventually make you go crazy), and then ask students to do a short bit of writing. They are to imagine that it's last night, and they are writing in their diaries (or these days, blogs) about what they did yesterday. "Dear Diary," they are to write. "Today this is what I did." (Often, I will give them an example from my own life, which typically is quite mundane, chronicling my day of teaching and grading papers.)

After they've written their diary entries, ask them to share their writing with each other in pairs. Then solicit volunteers to share their entries with the entire class, trying to limit this to no more than two or three.

At this point, ask students to imagine that yesterday morning, as soon as they awoke, they found a ring like that of Gyges. They are now to write a diary entry of what their day was like with the magic ring. (If necessary, I'll offer an example of my own, with tales of the new bike I lifted from the fancy bike shop in town, the trip I took to Paris for lunch, and my adventure sneaking into the White House Oval Office to listen to the president's secret meeting.)

.are these with each other in dyads and then, once more,
rs to read their entries to the entire class. Usually, more
ɔ for this than the original one, and it's fine to let these
ɔnger than in round 1 as well. Not surprisingly, most
students give accounts of the naughty and/or unethical things they did
with the magic ring; they talk about playing tricks on people, about stealing expensive items from stores and money from banks, and about doing
things—like driving cars very fast—that they are prevented from doing
by law. But perhaps unexpectedly, a good number of students also talk
about admirable actions they took, like stopping someone from being
bullied, or helping a homeless person, or capturing a fugitive from justice.

Have the class wonder together why we don't do these things—both
bad and good—in our everyday lives. Is the position argued for by the
"Ring of Gyges" story—that we're only good because we're afraid of
getting caught—correct? Do the examples of people using the ring for
good prove that wrong? Alternately, even if we would use the ring to do
good things sometimes, wouldn't we also use it for more selfish purposes? And wouldn't we eventually be corrupted by it?

This line of questioning can go on for a while, and usually students
are reasonably intrigued by it. The natural transition is to eventually
move on to the question of how we know what's right and wrong in the
first place, an issue explored in the next exercise.

LESSON PLAN: "LIFEBOAT" EXERCISE

Class activity ?

Topic/Question

Ethics/What is an ethical principle?

Age Group

Sixth grade and up

Time

About forty-five minutes

Materials

Pre-printed "characters" to pass out to each student (see below)

Description

The intent of this activity is to get students thinking about the role that principles play in moral reasoning—or, for that matter, reasoning in general. The goal is to encourage students to develop a principle (or at least a good reason) for a judgment they make and then to reflect upon that principle in order to modify it if necessary.

The activity itself is simple and fun; it's a "lifeboat" exercise in which teams of students work together to reach consensus on which member of the "lifeboat" they share will have to be sacrificed for the good of the others. The reason it's not *Survivor* television, though, is that it has a philosophical underpinning and requires students to articulate their reasons in a shared community of inquiry.

To begin the exercise, ask students to reflect on some moral judgment they've made. Have them write down the judgment and then try to explain the reason they made the judgment they did. So, for instance, a student once wrote, "It is wrong to steal money from your little brother to buy candy." And the reason she judged it so was because "I wouldn't want him to do that to me." Another student said, "You shouldn't punch little kids in the head." The reason, he said, was because it causes them pain and makes them cry. Usually, it works to have a short discussion about the kinds of reasons that students put forth for their judgments; this typically involves clarifying the difference between explanation and justification in ethical reasoning. As mentioned in chapter 3, an explanation is a psychological consideration; explanatory reasons refer to the causes of a person's beliefs. Justification is a philosophical consideration; justificatory reasons are presented in order to persuade others to accept your position, based on an appeal to reason.

Generally, though, it's not necessary to spend too much time on this; the main point for students to reflect upon is simply that our ethical judgments generally have some grounding; there's some sort of principle that we're applying when we engage in moral reasoning. The exercise that follows helps them think more carefully about such principles.

Divide students into groups of four or five. Explain that each group is a "lifeboat," and that students will be given characters to play in those lifeboats. Hand out to each student a description of the character he or she is playing. Here are the descriptions:

- You are a mailroom clerk in a large law firm. You are twenty-two years old and are planning to get your law degree when you graduate college. You are not married and have no children. You live at home with your parents.
- You are a front desk clerk at a local hotel. You are fifty-five years old and semi-retired. You have a twenty-year-old daughter and an eighteen-year-old son. Both are in college. You take care of your wife, who has a chronic illness.
- You are a construction worker. You are thirty years old and are married with three children. You hope to own your own construction business someday.
- You are a certified public accountant. You are forty-five years old and are married. You have two teenage children. You are active in your church and other community groups. You regularly volunteer at the local homeless shelter.
- You are a twelve-year-old student in sixth grade. You are the president of your class and have lots of friends. You hope to be a doctor when you grow up.
- You are a very successful attorney. You are forty-three years old and make over $200,000 a year. Your specialty is corporate law. You are married but don't have any children.
- You are a physician. Your specialty is pediatric medicine. You are thirty-five years old and are married with a three-year-old child.
- You are a schoolteacher. You are sixty years old and are planning on retiring soon. Your students are very fond of you and always enjoy your classes.
- You are a professional jewel thief. You make your living by stealing from very rich people, and you give part of the profits to a local food bank. You are twenty-seven, married, and have three children under the age of ten.
- You are a U.S. congressman or congresswoman. You are thirty-five years old and are married with two kids in elementary school. You are active in a number of community organizations that help the homeless.

- You are a homeless person. You are fifty-five years old and have been out of work for ten years. You are not married and have no children.

- You are a fast-food clerk. You are seventeen years old and are saving up for college. You live with your parents and have two younger siblings.

- You are the chief executive officer of a major corporation. You earn $1.5 million a year. Your company makes athletic shoes and manufactures them in foreign countries, which allows you to make a huge profit. You are fifty-five, divorced, and you share custody of your two teenage children.

- You are an eighty-five-year-old retired person. You live in a retirement home in Florida. You have twelve grandchildren and three great-grandchildren.

- You are a world-famous rock star. You have fans all around the world. You are twenty-six years old and are not married and have no children. You are extremely controversial as a musician and also have a bad drug habit.

- You are a six-month-old baby. You are your parents' first child and the first grandchild for your grandparents.

- You are a police officer. You are thirty, married, and have two young children.

- You are a welfare recipient and twenty-eight years old. You haven't worked in three years. You have six children, none of whom live with you.

- You are a college professor. You are thirty-three years old and are just starting out in your professional career. You plan to do research and write books on your specialty, which is ancient Greece.

- You are a sixteen-year-old high school student. You have been in trouble with the law a few times. You are thinking of dropping out and getting a job, even though your parents don't think you should.

- You are twenty-six years old and in jail on burglary charges, although you claim you are innocent of the crime. Before you went to jail, you were a social worker. You are married and have four children in elementary school.

- You are a newspaper journalist. You are twenty-eight years old and are recently married. Your interest is in investigative reporting, and you hope to make a career out of exposing fraud in government.

- You are an internationally famous horse trainer. You have personally trained a number of Kentucky Derby winners. You are forty-five years old and married with three college-age children.

- You are one of the world's leading experts in outdoor survival techniques. You are an excellent guide and know a good deal about how to survive in the wild. You are forty years old and single.
- You are a zookeeper. At your zoo, you are responsible for the care and feeding of the gorillas, who will die without you for their care. You are thirty-one years old and have no children.
- You are an eight-year-old student in third grade. You have two older siblings. You like to draw pictures and read books. When you grow up, you plan to be an architect.
- You are a biologist. You study a wide variety of animals and ecosystems. You are forty-four years old, married, and have one child, age ten.
- You are a nurse. You are forty-eight years old and have been a professional nurse for twenty-five years. You care a lot about your patients and are well liked by all of them.
- You are an airline pilot. You are forty-three years old and married with five children.
- You are a deep-sea commercial fisherman or fisherwoman. You know a lot about boats and navigation. You are thirty-one years old and married with no children.
- You are a world-famous professional athlete who makes about $10 million a year. You are twenty-seven years old and are single. You plan to retire from athletics soon and devote yourself to teaching children.
- You are an author of children's books. Millions of kids love your work and look forward to new volumes. You are forty-three years old and a single parent with one child.

Give a character description to each student (if the class is small, then you might give two descriptions to each student).

Explain that, as is the case in such lifeboat exercises, the boat each group is in is sinking. In order to save the rest of the people in the boat, one person from each boat must be sacrificed; otherwise, all will drown. Groups have to discuss among themselves and decide which person will be sacrificed. But—and this is the key point—groups have to work together to come to their decision; more importantly, all have to agree on the principle, or reason, by which the person who is to be sacrificed was chosen. And then, most important of all, the person who is to be sacrificed has to be able to articulate, to the rest of the class, why he or she was chosen—in particular, the principle that was used to make that choice.

It usually takes about ten minutes for the lifeboats to come to some agreement about who should be sacrificed. While students are wrangling over their decisions, wander around and listen to their discussions. Sometimes, if a group is really stuck, it helps to make students trade their characters. Participants can come to identify too strongly with the original character they've been given; making them switch sometimes gives them a new perspective that can move the discussion forward.

In any case, once all the groups have decided, go around, lifeboat by lifeboat, and hear what each group has to say. It has proven very effective to have each character introduce him- or herself and then have the person who is to be sacrificed explain why he or she was chosen. Write down on the board the principle or principles that were used to make the decision. Typically such principles are things like "whoever has lived the fullest life," or "whoever makes the least contribution to society," or "whoever is least likely to contribute to the good of the others in the boat," or "whoever has the least life potential."

Sometimes groups will insist that no one has a right to make such decisions and that the only fair thing to do is to draw straws or have everyone sacrifice him- or herself. This is a fruitful discussion to have, but try to set it aside at this point, emphasizing that the point is not to take on the overarching moral question of whether it's acceptable to make such life-or-death decisions. Rather, the focus is on trying to practice developing principles and reflecting upon them.

Then, after each group has gone, and each group's principle is listed on the board, explain that, as is the case in such exercises, the lifeboat continues to sink and another person must now be sacrificed. The good news, though, is that each group has already developed their principle, so this time it should be pretty easy to decide on who to sacrifice, just by applying the principle again. Set that task to the groups, with the caveat that, if their principle seems to yield a result that strikes them as unfortunate, mistaken, or immoral, they can modify their principle as needed, or even develop a brand-new one. Again, though, the person to be sacrificed needs to be able to explain why he or she was sacrificed, according to either the original principle or its modification.

During the explanations this second time, students usually talk a lot more about whether their principle was applied or not. Typically, some groups use their principle in a perfectly straightforward way, applying it to the "next in line"; other groups find that the original principle would force them to an outcome they are unwilling to accept—this is often sacrificing a youngster.

After two rounds, say that the boats are really sinking and that only one member of each boat can be saved. Here, typically, the original principles that each boat developed may be less helpful; nevertheless, it's still up to students to explain why they chose to save the person they did and to share that with the larger group.

Finally, as a capstone to the exercise, say that the rescue helicopter is coming but that only one individual can be saved. Have a large-group discussion about who that one remaining person should be. Typically, in the end, we vote on whom we want to save.

Usually, the six-month-old baby "wins," which is somewhat surprising, given the principles that most of the groups will have originally developed. But usually an interesting discussion ensues about why the baby ends up being the favored survivor. (It usually hinges on the emotional appeal of babies and the feeling most students have that they wouldn't want to be a survivor knowing that a baby died for them.) Sometimes, though, the forty-three-year-old children's book author "wins," on the basis of her fame and how many people love her books. (This seemed to happen more frequently before the final volume of the *Harry Potter* books came out; now that the full series is finished for all to read, the "J. K. Rowling" character doesn't elicit quite as much sympathy.)

LESSON PLAN: "WHAT DO RIGHTS LOOK LIKE?" EXERCISE

Topic/Question

Ethics/What is a right?

Age Group

Sixth grade and up

Time

About forty-five minutes

Materials

Pre-printed rights to pass out to each student (see below), and blank pieces of paper and crayons or colored pencils for each student to draw with

Description

This exercise is meant to explore the nature of rights in general, with an emphasis on inquiry into the rights of children. It's a fairly uncomplicated activity and can easily be completed in a typical fifty-minute class period. As an experience that combines individual and group work, it lends itself well to larger classes; in most classes where I've done the exercise, there were about thirty students.

Begin by wondering together what rights students currently have. Most groups understand that concept and find it easy to reel off rights that they allegedly possess. Some examples are easy: the right to life, the right to an education, the right to free speech, and so on. Others are more contentious: the right to medical care, the right to die, or the right to marry, for example. Talk a bit about the rights that students disagree on; this will lead naturally into the exercise, which can be positioned by saying something like "Well, okay, it's obvious that we're unclear on some of these supposed rights. Let's do an exercise that will help us get a better picture of what rights look like."

Begin the exercise by passing out to each student a different right that he or she presumably possesses. Students are allowed to look at the right they have been handed out, but they are not permitted to show their right to any of their classmates.

Here is the list of rights:

- You have the right to speak freely.
- You have the right to worship as you choose.
- You have the right to a free education.
- You have the right to eat candy.
- You have the right to be friends with whomever you want.
- You have the right to disagree with your teacher.
- You have the right to sit where you want in the lunchroom.

- You have the right to sit on the couch in class.
- You have the right to receive medical care if you get sick.
- You have the right to ride the bus.
- You have the right to hunt animals.
- You have the right to wear whatever clothes you want.
- You have the right to listen to the music of your choice.
- You have the right to go barefoot.
- You have the right to have as many children as you want.
- You have the right to *not* be friends with somebody.
- You have the right to dance.
- You have the right to sing.
- You have the right to *not* have anyone sit on your head.
- You have the right to privacy in your locker.
- You have the right to petition your school for changes.
- You have the right to *not* eat meat.
- You have the right to sleep in class.
- You have the right to make a cake.
- You have the right to live wherever you want.
- You have the right to a job.
- You have the right to enough money to live on even if you don't work.
- You have the right to inexpensive public transportation.
- You have the right to vote.
- You have the right to watch television.
- You have the right to stay up as late as you want.
- You have the right to pursue your own happiness.
- You have the right to disagree with your school principal.
- You have the right to get a tattoo.

(This list grew out of discussions in previous classes about rights. Some of them were contentious; not all students agreed that they had, for instance, the right to sleep in class. Still, the list contains a fairly representative sample of the rights that most of the students I was working with thought they had—or, at least, would like to think they had. The right to *not* have anyone sit on your head came out of a discussion inspired by Dr. Suess's *Yertle the Turtle*, which can be used as a tee-up or capstone to this exercise.)

In any case, once each student is given a right, ask them to take about ten to fifteen minutes to illustrate it on paper with crayons or colored pencils. Obviously, there is lot of variation in how much effort students put into their drawings. Some students draw extremely expressive pictures in full color; others sketch with stick figures in pencil. Don't put any constraints or conditions on their creativity here. Just ask that when they finish, they don't show their drawings to their fellow students or tell their classmates what right they have illustrated.

When everyone is done drawing (or at the end of the fifteen minutes or so), have each student write (in very small letters) on the back of their drawing what right they have illustrated.

The class in now broken into two teams. Ask students to name their teams; give them about a minute to do so, then write the team names on the board. Collect all the drawings, making sure to have them separated by teams into two stacks. Take a drawing of (let's say) the left-side stack and call on a student from the other team. He or she is given about twenty seconds to look at the drawing, which the facilitator can also describe as needed, and to guess what right it illustrates.

Should he or she correctly identify the right, that team earns a point. Then take a drawing from that team's stack, and, calling on the student from the first team who did the drawing you just observed, repeat the process.

Depending on the class, it can work to go through every drawing in both stacks. More typically, however, some subset of the drawings will be observed, at which point a winner is declared (or else a tie is achieved, due to creative scorekeeping on my part), and the next part of the exercise follows.

Pass out all the illustrations; students usually won't get their own drawing, but it's okay if they do. Organize the class into groups of four or five and have each group decide which of the rights in their group is the most important. Groups have to try to come to a consensus among themselves about this; if they really come to loggerheads over more than one, though, they can identify two that are equally important. Give them about ten minutes for this part of the exercise. During their discussions, go around the room and join in, asking questions and encouraging students to give the best reasons they can think of to support their positions.

The rights that typically emerge as important from this part of the exercise are as follows:

- You have the right to be friends with whomever you want.
- You have the right to disagree with your teacher.

- You have the right to receive medical care if you get sick.
- You have the right to listen to the music of your choice.
- You have the right to have as many children as you want.
- You have the right to *not* be friends with somebody.
- You have the right to live wherever you want.
- You have the right to a job.
- You have the right to vote.
- You have the right to pursue your own happiness.

On the blackboard, list the right (or rights) that each group has identified as most important. Then ask students to write down which of the listed rights is *most* important, and why. Give them about five minutes to do this. (The intent of writing at this point is just to help students collect their thoughts for the discussion that follows.)

Some sample answers (from a couple of sixth-grade classes) include those listed here:

- "The right to medical attention is the most important because if you don't have that right, people would get really sick and die, and then nobody would be around to have any rights at all."
- "The right to pursue your own happiness is most important because if you have that right, then you can do all the others, like vote, or listen to music, or have all the children you want."
- "The right to vote is the best one because without voting, there wouldn't be any rights at all."
- "The right to have kids is the most important because if people didn't have kids, there would be no people, and with no people there would be no rights."
- "The right to choose your own friends is the most important because who your friends are is one of the most important things in your life."
- "I think that the right of medical attention is most important, because if you didn't have medical attention, you could get hurt, or worse, die. Plus, the other ones are stupid."

Have a discussion to try to come to a consensus about which of the listed rights is the most important. Routinely, this discussion is excellent. Two or more rights often emerge as especially important; this leads students into a spirited discussion about which of these is the most crucial.

For instance, in one of the sixth-grade classes, students were pre.., evenly split over the right to vote and the right to pursue one's own happiness. Those who supported voting as most important argued that society could put the right to pursue happiness to a vote; consequently, voting rights would have to take precedence over happiness rights. Those who supported the right to pursue happiness argued that people wouldn't vote if it didn't make them happy, so obviously happiness took precedence.

In another class, students were split over the right to medical attention and the right to have as many children as you want. Basically, those who argued for the former emphasized that without the right to medical attention, people might be too ill or injured to exercise their rights. Those who argued for the latter pointed out that without children, there wouldn't be anyone around to have rights anyway. (This answer revealed some confusion about rights; students were assuming that the absence of a right meant that a person couldn't engage in that behavior at all as opposed to simply being unable to have that behavior protected in some way. Still, their reasoning, with this assumption, seemed sound.)

Finally, after your discussion, take a vote to decide which of the rights the class as a whole takes to be most important. (Typically, if the class has identified the right to vote as one of the important ones, someone points out the irony of *voting* on this decision.) Ask students to close their eyes and put their heads down on their desks to guarantee a secret ballot. Then have students cast their votes.

In the classes in which I've done this exercise, the right to pursue one's own happiness has won most often, followed by the right to medical attention, and the right to vote. Clearly, all of these represent extremely fundamental rights; what's been exciting for me in doing this exercise is not to have students come up with the "right" answer (as if there is one), but rather to see how students in a community of inquiry reason together to work toward a reasonable consensus about what rights are and which of them matter more than others. And I think this exercise does a pretty good job of making that possible.

Cl₄ss activity?

LESSON PLAN: THE "RED/GREEN" GAME

How should we treat each other?

Age Group

Fourth grade and up

Time

About thirty minutes

Materials

Two squares of paper, each with one side that is green and one side that is red (two pieces of construction paper, one red and one green, stapled back-to-back work well to make one square, but even a square of typing paper with magic marker coloring on either side is fine)

Description

This exercise is intended to get students thinking about the role of cooperation in ethical reasoning and behavior. It also functions as a model for a wide range of problems in ethics, especially those related to collective action. It's especially useful as a way to introduce challenges such as human-induced global climate change, health care allocation, and other similar social problems.

The exercise itself is a "prisoner's dilemma" game, although it's not necessary to talk about that beforehand—or even afterward, except perhaps with older students, say, high school and above. (The theory isn't essential to the success of the exercise but may be of interest to participants in higher grades.)

In any case, underlying the activity is the recognition that some contemporary philosophers, arguing in a broadly Hobbesian tradition, consider the purpose of ethical constraints on people's behavior to be in support of self-interest. We ought, for example, to be honest and fair because—in the long run—honesty and fairness enable us to get more of what we want out of life.

To illustrate this idea, a so-called prisoner's dilemma model is often used. In the prisoner's dilemma scenario, we see that straightforwardly acting in one's rational self-interest leads to an outcome that is less desirable for everyone involved. Ethical constraints on one's behavior—constraints that emphasize cooperation over competition—enable agents in a prisoner's dilemma to solve the dilemma in such a way that maximizes overall benefits for all parties involved.

Briefly, the prisoner's dilemma scenario goes something like this. You and a partner are, let's say, bank robbers. You have made a deal with each other that should you get caught in the act, neither of you will squeal on, or "rat out," your partner. Unfortunately for the two of you, you're caught by the police, who then take you into separate rooms to interrogate you. They try to get you to confess and incriminate your partner, giving each of you, unbeknown to the other, the following deal:

- If neither of you squeal, you'll both get six months in jail.
- If both of you squeal, you'll each get a year in jail.
- If you squeal and your buddy doesn't, you'll go free; he'll get ten years.
- Conversely, if he squeals and you don't, he'll go free; you'll get ten years.

Obviously, both of you will do better if you cooperate with each other and keep your original agreement not to squeal. But, unfortunately, each of you will do even better if you defect on your pact while your buddy cooperates. The difficulty is that you both know this, so no matter what the other person does, it's in your best interest to defect. What typically happens, therefore, in such situations, is that both parties defect, thereby doing worse than they would have had they both cooperated. This exercise is intended to demonstrate that dynamic in an interactive, engaging, and usually somewhat surprising way.

Begin by breaking the class into two teams of equal size. The teams line up facing each other. The player at the head of each line is given a paper square that is red on one side and green on the other. Explain to the students that each person in line will have a chance to compete against his or her counterpart in the opposing team's line.

In the game, there are only two rules, which are stated as follows: "There are only two rules in this game: No talking except when I say there is, and both teams try to score as many points as possible." After stating the rules, it's a good idea to pick someone to repeat the rules so that students begin hearing them again and again.

Then explain how points are to be scored: Players will stand back to back and show to you—standing in front of them—either the red side or the green side of their square. They will be awarded points depending upon the side of the square they show and the side their opponent shows. (I use the standard prisoner's dilemma matrix to award them.) Here's what to say:

- If you show green and your opponent shows green, you each get three points.
- If you show green and your opponent shows red, you get one point and your opponent gets four points.
- If you show red and your opponent shows green, you get four points and your opponent gets one point.
- If you both show red, you each get two points.

Then remind students of the rules: "No talking except when I say there is, and both teams try to score as many points as possible."

Make it a point to say no more than that. Point out that it's time to move into the "no talking" phase of the activity. The game then starts.

In the first round, players tend to try a variety of strategies—sometimes showing red, sometimes green. As the round goes on, though, it becomes apparent to team members that it behooves them to not show green; it is always (as is the case in collective-action problems like this) in their self-interested benefit to show red. Red dominates green in this game's theoretic matrix. By the end of the round, therefore, most players are showing red, and if they don't, their teammates usually moan.

At the end of the first round, tally up the teams' scores. Ask a student to remind the teams of the rules of the game (*no talking except when I say there is, and both teams try to score as many points as possible*). Then say this is a "talking" part and give them one minute to talk with their own team members to strategize for a second round. After doing so, again prohibit them from talking and the second round begins.

The results are fairly predictable. All players show red, and as a result, their scores, both as individual teams and as a group, tend to be lower than round 1. (Here, they are averaging two points per interaction, whereas in round 1, since sometimes they scored 1 or 4, the average was usually closer to 2.5.)

Demonstrate to students they are actually doing worse the more they play. Isn't the point of the game to maximize their scores? Here, ask a student to remind the teams of the rules of the game, which you can restate as needed: "No talking except when I say there is, and both teams try to score as many points as possible."

Now give teams one minute to strategize not only with their own team members but also with members of the opposing team. About half the time, students choose to talk across team boundaries; don't insist that they do so, but do encourage it. At the end of this round, talk is again stopped, and a third round of the game ensues.

Generally, in this round, all players show green. (Not always, though; it's been my experience that students in advanced programs have a tougher time cooperating than students in regular programs. Also, it's not unusual that about halfway through, some student—usually a boy—will show red, setting off a chain reaction of red being shown.) But usually, teams do cooperate, and each side averages three points per interaction; players thus see how their team does better by cooperating with the other team.

Then debrief the game in two ways. First, discuss situations in real life that have this sort of dynamic. Usually, students bring up all sorts of classic collective-action problems: adhering to pollution control standards, limiting fishing, using high-occupancy-vehicle lanes, refraining from cheating on tests. Talk about how individuals and groups in such collective-action problems can work together to maximize their collective benefit.

Then ask students to perform a brief writing project that answers two questions:

- What did you learn in this game?
- How can you use it in your life?

Students take five minutes or so and write down their answers. They then each have the option of reporting their answer to their classmates. Most do, and their answers tend to be quite moving, as they explain ways in which they can do better by cooperating with others in the future.

I have played this game with students as young as fourth grade and as old as college-level. Although the discussion in the debrief tends to be more or less sophisticated, the "A-ha!" that students get about the value of cooperation is equally powerful at all of these levels.

A very clear principle emerges from the game and discussion—we are more likely to get what we want by cooperating than by single-mindedly pursuing our limited self-interest. This principle represents a strong underlying foundation upon which to build further ethical understanding. It's also a workable principle to apply in choosing between alternatives in real life.

You can then wonder together about what sort of incentives or punishments might be in order to ensure that people are more likely to cooperate; some say this is where ethics has its foundation.

LESSON PLAN: "HAND DEALT"

Topic/Question

Ethics/Is life fair?

Age Group

Fifth grade and up

Time

About forty-five minutes

Materials

Pre-printed cards in three categories: relationship, occupation, and dwelling (see below) and paper clips

Description

This exercise is intended to explore the question "What is fairness?" by giving students an opportunity to assume different characters in a community and wonder about the most equitable way to distribute social benefits to all members of that society.

The late philosopher John Rawls is famous for exploring the relationship between justice and fairness. In his seminal *A Theory of Justice*, Rawls argues that the guiding principles of justice are those that free and rational persons concerned to further their own interests would accept in an initial position of equality.[2] The choice that rational people would make in this hypothetical situation of equal liberty determines, for Rawls, the principles of justice. A key concept in Rawls's account of justice as fairness is that—when choosing these principles—no one knows what his or her place in society is. Agents choose the principles of justice behind a "veil of ignorance" that ensures that no one is prejudicially favored in the distribution of natural assets or social benefits. Presumably, fairness— and thus justice—is guaranteed by this arrangement.

The intent of this exercise is to re-create the Rawlsian model through an exploration of the question "Is life fair?"

Begin simply by pondering the question "Is life fair?" Ask students what they think. Routinely, two themes emerge. On the one hand, most students will opt for the view that life isn't fair. They will cite examples from the larger societal perspective, such as the observation that some people have the good fortune to be born in relatively comfortable situations in the United States, for instance, while others have the misfortune to be born in very difficult and challenging circumstances, like in impoverished areas of Africa or India. Or they will offer examples from their own lives, such as "My brother, who's younger than me, gets to stay up as late as I do, even though when I was his age, I had to go to bed earlier." Responses such as this indicate support for the position that life is not fair.

On the other hand, some students will argue that life is fair based on the view that everyone has the same opportunity to respond to their fortunes or misfortunes as they see fit. "I may not be as rich as Bill Gates," a student will say, "but I have just as much a chance of being happy as he does; it's up to me to decide."

During this phase of the exercise, there's no need to achieve a consensus; mainly, it's just an opportunity to hear what students have to say. If the class seems eager to start debating the issue, try to steer them toward the upcoming activity, in which the question of whether life is fair will be dealt with at length.

To begin the activity, students are dealt cards that assign them a job, a relationship, and a living situation. Make the point that in everyone's life, these three categories exist, even if the category itself might be empty—as in the case of someone being unemployed or homeless. (A complete list of cards is provided at the end of this section.)

In any case, the cards are dealt out randomly to each student. The relationship cards are given first and determine, based on whether the character dealt is single or married, whether a student will receive one occupation card or two. (Single characters receive one; married characters receive two.) Depending on the hand dealt, a character might be, for example, a married couple with three children, with one parent being a janitor and the other a sales clerk, living in a two-bedroom apartment.

Once students have their identities assigned, they are charged with writing a short biography of their characters. Sometimes odd combinations result, as in the case of a character who has a good job but ends up homeless. It's useful for students to imagine how such scenarios are possible.

Students are then given the opportunity to introduce their characters to the class. Ideally, every participant will avail him- or herself of this; no one is required to do so, though. For what it's worth, however, nearly every student, especially in the lower grades, opts to do so.

After each student presents his or her character, ask, "From the perspective of your character, would you say life is fair?" or "Would say that life has dealt you a fair hand?" Not surprisingly, students who've been dealt a desirable hand tend to respond that life is fair; those whose lives are less desirable tend to say that it isn't.

When the entire class has made their introductions, follow up on the fairness question. Ask, "Would everyone who thinks they were dealt a pretty good or better life please raise your hand?" When those students have done so, say, "Okay, those of you with your hands in the air, leave your hands raised if, from the perspective of your character, you would say that life is fair." Typically, most of these students will keep their hands up. Point this out to the class, and then request that all hands be lowered.

Now say, "Would those of you who think you were dealt a not-so-good hand or worse please raise your hands?" When those students have done so, again say, "Those of you with your hands in the air, leave your hands raised if, from the perspective of your character, you would say that life is fair." Typically, most of these students will lower their hands. Point this out to the class and wonder aloud, "So, what's up with this? How come the people who were dealt pretty good or better lives said that life was fair, while those who got not-so-good or worse lives said life was unfair? What is fairness, anyway?"

The students might ponder that together a bit, but the promise is that the next part of the activity will give them a better idea of what fairness actually is.

Hold up a handful of different colored cards. On these are a number of societal benefits—things that could help improve peoples' lives. These benefits include job training, new housing, educational subsidies, even a lottery win. Ask the class to strategize methods to allocate social benefits in ways that would be most fair. Students brainstorm a list of principles for allocating these benefits, which are written on the board. Some typical alternatives include allocation by merit, by need, at random, or to people with blond hair. In general, there is spirited discussion about the best way to allocate benefits, the point being to simply list as many possible principles for distributing the benefits as students can think of, even if some of those principles sound outlandish. Encourage students to come up with principles that they themselves might not endorse.

It can also be useful to gently push students to offer possibilities that might seem manifestly unfair, such as giving all the benefits to one particular character; again, the goal here is to list as many possible principles on the board as students can come up with.

Participants are then asked to set aside everything they know about their characters. To do this, hand out a paper clip to each student. They clip their cards together and the cards are collected. Explain that, presently, their lives will be passed back, but no one knows which life they will receive. Consequently, no one knows whether, for example, they are a married schoolteacher making $30,000 a year or a single homeless person living on welfare. Behind this "veil of ignorance," what turns out to be the fairest, most just way to allocate benefits?

The character of the discussion changes radically. No longer are students solely focused on what they can get. Rather, they are interested in designing and selecting principles that allocate social benefits in a far more just and equitable way. The principles that emerge from this discussion can then be applied in their own lives—in the classroom, on the playground, and with their families and friends.

Usually the principles that prevail are broadly need-based. Typically, students come to agree that benefits should be passed out to people who are homeless, or who make the least money and have the most kids, or who are unemployed or living on welfare. Sometimes, though, students want to assert that handing out benefits randomly is the fairest method of doing so.

Pass back the lives that have been collected, trying to make sure that no one gets the life they had originally. The class can then "test" the principles for distribution that students came up with by passing out the benefits to the characters whose situations fit those principles. Usually, a pretty good discussion follows in which students wonder together about whether the principles they generated for distributing the benefits really are fair. Often, students remain satisfied that they are; other times, the general consensus is that, in practice, the principles don't really work. If that's the view, the class can explore further why that's the case, and whether there is any more fair way they could have come up with.

Then hold up cards on which are a number of bad things: death in the family, job loss, long-term disability, and so forth. The question is posed as to what is a fair way to hand out the bad things. Generally, students tend to converge on the view that bad things should be passed out randomly, since that's how it happens in real life. However, sometimes classes want to argue that the rich people should get them, since they will be better able to handle them. I've even had one or two classes claim that the fairest way to pass out the bad things is to give them to the worst off, since that's the real world, or to give them to anyone who previously received benefits, as a way to balance the good with the bad.

As a consequence of this exercise, students develop a more sophisticated understanding and appreciation for the relationship between justice and fairness, as well as an increased ability to apply the principles of justice for themselves.

Here is the list of cards, according to categories. (There can be more than one of each in the relationship and dwelling categories.)

Relationship Cards

- Single parent, one child
- Single parent, two children
- Two parents, four children
- Two parents, two children
- Single, no children
- Two parents, one child
- Single parent, three children
- Two parents, seven children
- Two parents, three children
- Single parent, seven children
- Two parents, no children

Occupation Cards

- Bank executive, $125K/year
- Nurse's aide, $20K/year
- Front-desk clerk, $17K/year
- Police officer, $40K/year
- Biologist, $35K/year
- Owner, rock-climbing gym, $10K/year
- AFDC recipient, $6K/year
- Computer analyst, $100K/year
- Zookeeper, $38K/year
- Professional salesperson, $50K/year
- Contractor, $36K/year
- Trucker, $65K/year
- U.S. Army private, $13K/year
- Accountant, $30K/year
- Bartender, $15K/year
- High school teacher, $40K/year
- Computer consultant, $190K/year
- Attorney, $206K/year
- Dishwasher, $7K/year
- Physician, $190K/year
- Corporate CEO, $1.5 million/year
- Hotel worker, $10K/year
- Fruit packer, $8K/year
- Systems technician, $40K/year
- Janitor, $35K/year
- Graphic artist, $50K/year
- Architect, $60K/year
- Forklift operator, $21K/year
- Plumber, $80K/year
- Engineer, $76K/year
- Management consultant, $110K/year
- Scientist, $80K/year
- Electrician, $65K/year
- Computer programmer, $95K/year
- Chiropractor, $125K/year
- Chemical engineer, $110K/year
- Owner, printing company, $26K/year

- Mailroom clerk, $18K/year
- Taxi driver, $25K/year
- Artist, $6K/year
- Research assistant, $20K/year
- Actor/actress, $15K/year
- Farmer, $35K/year
- Psychologist, $60K/year
- Motel owner, $35K/year
- College professor, $35K/year
- Realtor, $45K/year
- Office clerk, $20K/year
- Mechanic, $25K/year
- Laborer, $10K/year
- Social worker, $25K/year
- City councilperson, $30K/year
- U.S. Air Force lieutenant, $75K/year
- Unemployed person, $0/year
- Journalist, $55K/year
- Part-time store clerk, $5K/year
- Health care attendant, $9K/year
- Landscaper, $26K/year
- Store owner, $10K/year
- Waiter/waitress, $20K/year
- Firefighter, $35K/year
- Construction worker, $16K/year
- Record store clerk, $20K/year
- Fast-food cashier, $15K/year
- Barista, $24K/year
- Day care provider, $15K/year

Dwelling Cards

- Loft apartment
- Two-room apartment
- Two-room basement apartment
- Two-bedroom mobile home
- Live with relatives in a three-bedroom house
- Studio apartment
- Six-bedroom house

- Live with friends in a two-bedroom house
- One-room residence hotel
- Homeless
- Live in car
- Three-bedroom house
- One-bedroom apartment
- Live in school bus
- One-bedroom guest house
- Four-bedroom house
- Share two-bedroom apartment with a family of four
- Share two-bedroom apartment with three friends
- Two-bedroom condo
- Five-bedroom house with twenty-five acres

Benefits Cards

- Win lottery, $50K
- Job training program, new job
- Cash in stocks, $50K
- College scholarship, new job
- Inherit new home, four-bedroom house
- New job, salary increase of $50K/year
- Graduate school scholarship, new job

Bad Things Cards

- Car stolen, can't get to work, fired
- Drug addiction, lose job and home
- Mental illness, lose job
- Burglary, lose $50K
- Death in family, lose job
- Medical emergency, lose job
- Fire, lose home

Fifth grade and up

Time

About thirty minutes

Materials

Slips of paper listing various roles and responsibilities (see below) and a bag of candy

Description

Begin the exercise by holding up a bag of candy (make sure you have enough for at least one piece for every student) and asking, "What's the fair way to distribute the candy in this bag? Who should get a piece?"

Usually, students will agree that everyone should get the same number of pieces. (Occasionally, a student will—usually half in jest—claim that he or she ought to get the whole bag; this naturally doesn't fly with his or her classmates, and a discussion about why it's not right can ensue.)

After talking about a fair way to distribute the sweets, pass out the candy according to the decision of the group. After giving students a few moments to enjoy their treat, ask, "Is everyone getting the same thing always the fair way? Are there situations in which it's okay for people to be treated differently?"

Field responses and then segue into the roles and responsibilities exercise as follows.

Ask four volunteers to come to the front of the classroom. Explain that they are going to be working together to build a house. Each of them, though, has different tools. Pass out to each student a slip of paper with a different description of the tools he or she has. Ask them to read aloud what they've received. Here is what they've got:

- You have a bulldozer and a dump truck. You are an expert in the use of these machines.
- You have a full collection of hand tools like hammers, drills, and screwdrivers. You are an expert in the use of these tools.
- You have a huge supply of bricks and cement. You are an expert bricklayer and cement mixer.
- You have all the paints and brushes anyone could need. You are an expert painter.

Now ask students who they think should do what when the house is being built, and why. Usually it's pretty obvious, but the discussion can be fairly interesting as the class gets into talking about why so-and-so should do such-and-such. (It's also not unprecedented that students will say, for instance, that the painter ought to help do brick-laying, for example, as a way to learn new skills.)

As this discussion dies down, bring four different students to the front of the room and pass to them slips that read as follows:

- You are the world's greatest dessert chef.
- You are the world's greatest dishwasher.
- You are the world's greatest soup-maker.
- You are the world's greatest sandwich-maker.

Now say something like "Okay, it's time to make lunch for everyone. Who should do what?" Again, the discussion is likely to be pretty straightforward, with the class generally agreeing that the tasks should be divvied up according to expertise. (Again, this isn't always the case; sometimes students argue that people should be expected to do whatever is needed or that everyone ought to get good at everything. But most of the time, the consensus is that it's good for everyone if everyone does what he or she does best.)

Time permitting, do one more iteration. This time, bring five students to the front and pass out slips that read as follows:

- You are the world's best rebounder.
- You are the world's best shot-blocker.
- You are the world's best three-point shooter.
- You are the world's best passer.
- You are the world's best free-throw shooter.

Obviously, the question now is "What's the best way for this basketball team to play?" And again, pretty much just as obviously, students will respond that the players who are good at a given skill ought to focus on that skill. It's worth talking some about why; there might be different reasons to consider, ranging from something like "If everyone does what they're good at, the team will win" to "People have more fun if they do the thing they're good at." In any case, by this third iteration the class will have explored in some depth their positions on when it's appropriate (if at all) for people to have different responsibilities given that they have different skills and abilities.

At this point, pass out to all students slips of paper with the phrase "What I do best is _____," and ask them to fill in the blank. When they've done so, bring a group of four students (randomly chosen) to the front of the room. Ask each student to read his or her slip of paper. Then wonder aloud, "If you were building a house, who should do what?" Compare the answers in this discussion to those from the earlier example. What's similar? What's different? Why?

Do the same thing with different groups for the lunch-making and basketball-playing examples. Again, compare similarities and differences and probe together with students as to why they've answered as they have.

Finally, get everyone back in their seats and have each student read his or her slip out loud. Then have a large-group discussion focused on the question "Given our skills and abilities, who should do what in our classroom? What's the fair way to divvy up the tasks?" This often leads to an interesting contrast with the other discussions, although sometimes students will want to assert that since they're all good at different things, they all should have different kinds of assignments in the classroom.

The hope is that the class has begun to explore whether fairness always means that everyone should get the same thing. Are there cases in life where it's fair to give some people more (or different things) than others? Often, students will give examples like handicapped parking spaces or extra time in test-taking for people with learning disabilities. (These examples are often contentious; with older students, it's not unusual for the debate over affirmative action to emerge here, with all its complexities and challenges.)

At the end of this discussion, it works to do a fill-in-the-blank "poem," where students fill in this sentence: "With my special talents, one thing I

can do to make the world a little better is _____." Here ~~are~~
answers from a fourth-grade class:

- One thing I can do to make the world a little better
  friends.
- One thing I can do to make the world a little better is be nice to my
  brother.
- One thing I can do to make the world a little better is share my toys.
- One thing I can do to make the world a little better is play basketball.
- One thing I can do to make the world a little better is draw and
  paint.

LESSON PLAN: ANTS AND CHOCOLATE

Topic/Question

Ethics/How should we treat nonhuman animals?

Good for class

Age Group

Fifth grade and up

Time

About twenty minutes

Materials

A bag of Hershey's Kisses

Description

This activity is meant to get students thinking about animal rights.
The goal is to tease out their intuitions about what obligations human
beings have to nonhuman animals, and whether those obligations change
depending on the properties of the particular nonhuman animals under
consideration.

It's a simple exercise, but it requires some suspension of disbelief on
the part of students. Ask them to take seriously what they are going to be
told, and urge them to believe what they will hear, unbelievable as it
sounds.

ᴊegin the exercise by passing out Hershey's Kisses to each student. ᴊell them they will be allowed to eat it in a moment should they so desire, but they need to hear something about how the candy is made first.

Explain it this way: "Hershey's has long been a leader in alternative energy production, and they have a very novel way of producing electricity to run the machines that make Hershey's Kisses. The way it works is that some miles from the chocolate production, in a completely separate and sterile facility, the Hershey's company produces electricity by taking ants, putting them in this great big sealed chamber, and squishing them. (I admit that I don't understand the technology, but I do know that it's pretty effective; it takes the squishing of about one hundred ants to produce a bag of Hershey's Kisses.) It's important to understand that the ants are not taken from the wild; they are raised humanely in ant farms (ha-ha) and then squished instantly and painlessly."

The question, though, for students to consider is this: "Knowing that approximately one hundred ants had to die in order for this bag of Hershey's Kisses to be produced—that's about two ants per piece—do you have any qualms about eating the candy? If so, don't eat it, but if not, it's yours to consume."

The class usually has a pretty lively discussion about whether it's morally acceptable to eat the candy given that so many ants had to die. Most students don't have a problem with eating the chocolate. They point out that the ants have already died; whether one eats the candy or not won't bring them back. Or they explain that, as a matter of fact, from an environmental standpoint, it's actually a good thing, since no fossil fuels are burned to create the electricity.

Sometimes, students say that they hate ants and are glad to see them die. Others mention that since the ants weren't taken from the wild, since they were raised for this purpose, there's nothing morally questionable about eating the chocolate. On the other hand, students who resist eating the chocolate will point out that candy is a luxury; it's not as if we need chocolate to live (some students will debate that). Killing a living thing just for a luxury item is wrong, they will contend, so it's unacceptable to eat the chocolate. Besides, others will chime in, ants are an important part of the planetary ecosystem; we ought not to be killing them, even if they aren't harvested from the wild.

When these issues have been explored in sufficient detail, pass out another piece of candy to all the students who ate their original one. Then say that the business about the ant-squishing was just a joke: "Hershey's doesn't really squish ants to make electricity; actually, they squish laboratory rats—little white rats, bred especially for this purpose. Now the rats, of course, are more efficient than the ants; each squished rat produces enough electricity to make an entire bag of Hershey's Kisses. So each piece is only about 1/100 or so responsible for the rat's death. Now, who wouldn't want to eat their candy knowing this?"

Again, a good discussion usually ensues. Typically, a few more students resist eating the chocolate at this stage. They point out that rats experience pain, or that people have rats as pets, or that rats are cute. On the other hand, other students note that rats are used in experimentation, that they are pests, and that since the rats are killed painlessly, there's nothing wrong with using them this way.

Finally, when this discussion dies down, hand out a fresh piece of chocolate to all students who ate theirs, and again admit it was all a ruse: "Hershey's doesn't squish rats for electricity; actually, they squish kittens and puppies. But these animals are very efficient; it only takes one kitty or puppy to generate enough electricity for about one hundred bags of Hershey's Kisses. So any one piece hardly is responsible for the death of any given kitty or puppy."

At this point, many, if not most, students refuse to eat the chocolate. Usually, the predominant reasons are that kittens and puppies are cute and that they are pet animals. This, though, often leads into an interesting conversation about why we consider them pets and what that means. Usually someone mentions (especially in higher grades) that in some countries, dogs are eaten by humans, so what's the problem?

This naturally segues into a broader discussion of what our responsibilities to nonhuman animals are in general. Students regularly point out that since so many of us eat cows and pigs, why should we be upset that kittens and puppies are killed for making chocolate? By contrast, though, students will again point out that chocolate is a luxury, so we should resist killing them for something unnecessary.

Sometimes, if the mood of room seems open to it and time permits, I'll do one last version of the thought experiment. Hershey's Kisses are handed out once more to the willing participants. I'll admit that the story about the kittens and puppies wasn't true either. "Actually, Hershey's generates power by the squishing of . . . you guessed it: human infants. Of course, they are brain-damaged (there's no chance of them ever developing full cognitive abilities; indeed, they'll never be 'smarter' than a cat or a dog); and they're orphans (so no one who loves them will miss them). Would anyone be willing to eat their candy knowing that human beings (albeit damaged and abandoned ones) had to die?"[3]

Usually, no students will consent, but the reasons they tend to give are worthy of discussion. Most will say that it's wrong simply because the victim is human. But when the class begins to probe what it is about humans that make them special from an ethical standpoint, it's much harder for students to articulate a reason. This is philosopher Peter Singer's point: If the only reason for granting human beings special moral status is because they are human beings, then, arguably, we are guilty of what Singer calls "speciesism," analogous to racism or sexism. Generally, students understand this point, although many will disagree that there's anything inherently wrong with being a speciesist. The question of whether it's okay to kill humans in order to make chocolate remains pretty settled; the question of whether it's morally acceptable to kill animals, by contrast, remains quite open.

Rarely do we come to some sort of classroom consensus as to whether it's right or wrong to eat the chocolate if certain animals had to die. But, of course, that's not the point. What's valuable is the rich exploration of ideas that the exercise stimulates. (Students usually don't mind getting chocolate to eat either.)

LESSON PLAN: FISH AND CANDY

Topic/Question

Ethics/How should environmental resources be sustained?

Age Group

Sixth grade and up

Time

About thirty minutes

Materials

A large bag of individually wrapped candies like peppermints, jaw-breakers, or gumballs, two sets of chopsticks, two plastic drinking cups, and a stopwatch or watch with a second hand

Description

This exercise is intended to get participants thinking about environmental issues, especially issues around sustainability and our obligations when it comes to managing a shared commons. It was originally developed by classroom teacher Jean Hansen, who was my teaching assistant for several years in the University of Washington's "Summer Challenge" program. I've made some modifications to it, but much of what is here is still her original idea.

In this activity, students are split into two "tribes" of people who live around a lake and take their sustenance from the fish in those waters.

After organizing students into these two tribes (and, of course, encouraging both sides to come up with a name for their tribe), draw out a lake on the floor of the classroom using masking tape. Put a bunch of wrapped candy into the lake, about twice as many pieces as there are students participating in the activity. Students are given the basic background of their situation and asked to choose a designated fisherperson for their tribe. It is then explained to them that in a moment, the fishing season will begin, and in order for tribe members to survive the year, their designated fisherperson must catch at least one fish (piece of candy) for each member of the tribe. If the fisherperson catches fewer fish than the number of members of the tribe, the tribespeople without a fish die. If a fisherperson catches more fish than members of the tribe, new members (or previously dead ones) can be added to the living.

The wrinkle here is that the only tool that the designated fisherperson has to catch fish is a set of chopsticks; fisherpeople are only allowed to "pluck" candy, and they cannot go into the water to fish.

The fishing season starts; it lasts twenty seconds. Depending on the skill of the fisherperson with the chopsticks, it usually happens that most, but not all, of the tribe members get a piece of candy and "survive" into the next year.

Then replenish the lake with candy, adding a piece or two into the lake for each piece currently in it.

A second twenty-second fishing season is then "opened"; this time, though, fisherpersons can put one foot into the water, and they can also "brush" fish from the lake. Typically, this is more efficient, and usually enough fish are caught to feed all tribe members. Again, afterward, replenish the lake. Usually, it's still pretty healthy with fish.

A third fishing season is opened; this time, fisherpersons are each given a cup into which they can shovel fish with their chopsticks. Typically, this is far more efficient—so much so that the level of fish (that is, candy) in the lake is depleted to such an extent that even when new "fish" are added before the next round, their overall numbers will be much reduced.

Then it's time for a fourth season. This time, fisherpersons can go into the lake and scoop with their cups. Typically, the fishery is devastated, so that even when new "fish" are added, only a few remain; thus, the overall numbers are not replenished, and when the fifth season comes around, there aren't enough fish for tribe members to survive.

At this point, the class talks about strategies for what could have been done differently in the fourth season to avoid this calamity and how we could have made sure that people abided by those strategies.

To test that out, replenish the lake to fourth-season levels and open another season. (About half the time I do this activity, depending on the students, they behave sustainably; the other half of the time, the same mistakes are made. Either of these outcomes leads to interesting discussions about sustainability, fairness, and environmental degradation.)

Another option for the game is to start again with a single fisherperson per tribe; in order to expand their tribes' membership, fisherpersons have to catch a sufficient number of fish in each round to add tribe members. This can add a dimension of competition to the game as teams try to maximize their membership; it also simulates a common real-world dynamic since, for the most part, the size of social groups does tend to expand in response to the available food resources.

In both cases, though, students can keep all the candy they catch; sometimes this leads to an interesting real-world problem of fair distribution. What has been fascinating to observe is the degree to which students will translate what they experienced in the exercise into how they divvy up the candy. I wouldn't say that it necessarily makes them more likely to share, but I have observed that their conversations about what to do are sometimes more involved.

NOTES

1. Plato, *The Republic*, book 2, translated by B. Jowett (New York: Modern Library, n.d.).

2. John Rawls, *A Theory of Justice* (Cambridge, MA: Harvard University Press, 1971), 11.

3. This example broadly references Peter Singer's thought experiment about the moral acceptability of doing medical research on higher primates.

SEVEN

What Is the Meaning of Life?

I joke with students that you can't take a philosophy class without asking the question "What is the meaning of life?" And although I'm kidding, there's an element of truth to my claim. Arguably, it's the biggest of the "big" questions in philosophy, and something is missing from our philosophical inquiry if we don't take it on.

The following group of exercises, therefore, is meant to help us interrogate the topic of life's meaning. I never promise students that we'll find *the* answer; I do, however, express confidence that the search for it will be intriguing.

LESSON PLAN: WHAT'S WORTH DOING?

Topic/Question

Existentialism/What is the meaning of life?

Age Group

Sixth grade and up

Time

About twenty minutes

Materials

Pieces of paper and pens or pencils for each student to write with

Description

This exercise is intended to get participants thinking about value, especially as it pertains to the value of things that we do. In high school and college classes, students typically will preface the exercise by reading a selection from Bertrand Russell's widely anthologized "The Value of Philosophy," but that isn't required. In this essay, Russell argues that the value of philosophy is to be found not in the answers it provides, but rather in the questions it encourages us to think about. In doing so, he opens up a distinction between intrinsic value (things that are valuable in and of themselves) and instrumental value (things that are valuable because they enable us to achieve some other value). The hoped-for outcome from this activity is that students will develop a better understanding of these concepts, and that they will come to ponder together the degree to which philosophy, as a discipline and a practice, has either.

Begin the exercise by posing the question "What's worth doing?" Students are then asked to write down ten things they consider worthwhile. Encourage them to be honest with themselves and really think about the question. Emphasize that there's not a "right" answer, nor are they expected to offer suggestions that would necessarily be approved by their parents and teachers; the point is for them to think seriously about what they really consider worth doing, no matter what that is.

When they've got their lists of ten, ask them to partner up and share their lists with each other. Typically, they list things like "traveling," "getting an education," "sleeping," "spending time with friends and family," and "updating my Facebook page." Based on what their partner says, students may then modify or add to their own lists.

Introduce the distinction between intrinsic and instrumental value. Have students look at their lists of what's worth doing and ask themselves which sort of value they believe applies to the various activities they've listed. It's typical to engage, at this point, in a general discussion of the distinction, and it's not uncommon for students to find the difference somewhat muddled. This is fine. It's not important to agree about whether a given activity is intrinsically or instrumentally valuable, or even whether it's always possible to make the distinction. The goal is simply that students begin to develop an awareness of the distinction and an initial fluency in making it.

Next, ask students to imagine that they've gone to their doctor, who has informed them that they only have five years to live. Looking at their lists, are there any activities they've listed that they would no longer consider worth doing? Encourage students to share those activities with the larger group and talk about them. Typically, there will be a few things that students mention at this point; usually, they are activities that have long-term instrumental value, like getting an education or starting a career.

Now ask students to imagine that their doctor has told them they only have a year to live. Are there any other activities they would then remove from their list? Again, ask for students to offer up their choices and talk more about them.

Proceed to continue shortening the time frame, to six months, then a month, then a week; finally, ask students to imagine that they only have twenty-four hours to live: Which of the remaining activities would they still consider worth doing?

Typically, the kinds of things that remain are activities like spending time with family, giving praise to God, and (occasionally) sleeping. These are activities that students consider intrinsically valuable. Sometimes a few students will want to argue that, if you only have a day to live, then nothing is worth doing. This can be an interesting discussion as well.

The typical upshot of the exercise is that students have developed a better vocabulary for discussing value and have thought a bit about what they consider valuable and why. This strikes me as a worthwhile outcome, one with both intrinsic and instrumental value.

LESSON PLAN: "WHAT IS THE MEANING OF LIFE?" GAME

Topic/Question

Existentialism/What is the meaning of life?

Age Group

Sixth grade and up

Time

  About forty-five minutes

Materials

  A plastic bag containing three paper clips, a marble, four slide mounts, two bendable straws, and a pencil for each group of three to four students, and a sealed envelope with a blank sheet of paper inside (other items can be used; it doesn't really matter what you give to students as long as every group gets the same items)

Description

  This exercise is intended to explore the question of "What is the meaning of life?"—a question most students expect to be included in any philosophy class. Underlying it is an existentialist perspective, although that's not something that needs to be made explicit unless the exercise is being done with high school or college students, and then only after the exercise is completed.

  To begin the activity, pose the question "What is the meaning of life?" Students do a free-write about this, and the class will discuss their answers. Then explain that they will do a short exercise to delve more deeply into the question.

  Break students up into teams of three or four. Hand out to each team a plastic bag with the following items inside: three paper clips, four slide mounts, two bendable straws, a pencil, and a marble. (Other items can be substituted; I like using slide mounts because students often have never seen them, but I think cardboard squares could be substituted easily enough.)

  Tell the groups that they have fifteen minutes to create a game using the items they have just received. Hold up the sealed envelope and explain that the directions for how the pieces are *really* meant to be used are inside; their task, as teams, is to create a game that is closest to the directions as they are written.

  Teams then work together to create their games. At the conclusion of the fifteen minutes (or more, if necessary), each team presents their game, using the following model:

- Name of the game
- How the game starts/ends
- How many players
- One fun fact about the game

As teams describe their games (and typically, demonstrate them as well), write down on the board the name of each game. Once all the teams have presented, vote (as a class) on which game students think is most likely to be closest to the directions as they are written.

The team who wins the vote is given the envelope and told that, in a moment, one of their team members will open it and read the directions. Before doing that, however, explain to students that they are going to do a "phenemonological investigation." Refer briefly here to the twentieth-century philosophical movement called phenomenology, pointing out that the phenomenologists are interested in carefully examining specific phenomena, or experiences. They talk about "bracketing" an experience or event in order to study it fully. That's what students will do, in a moment, when they find out what the "real" directions are.

When the directions are revealed, students will have one minute to do a free-write about what they experience upon discovering those directions. Have students take out a piece of paper and ready their pencils.

The directions are then opened up and "read."

Of course, the directions are nothing more than a blank piece of paper. Students see this, and then take to writing for one minute.

At the conclusion of that minute, ask students to share their phenomenological investigations. Typically, their reactions fall into two main camps. Some students say they feel cheated, or bummed out, or angry that there are no real directions. They will never know, they say, whether their game was close to the way the pieces are meant to be used or not. Other students express relief, or a sense of freedom, or even joy that there are no "real" directions. They say they're glad because this means that any game is as good as any other and that we're all free to make up the game as we see fit.

The connection to existentialism here is pretty straightforward. On the one hand, we experience, upon finding out that there is no pre-set meaning to be found in the world, what Sartre calls "anguish," "abandonment," and "despair." At the same time, though, we are radically free to create a life that is meaningful to us, even in a meaningless universe.

It's generally pretty easy to get a discussion about this going among students; students like to talk about whether life has meaning, and this exercise provides a framework for those conversations to take place. The dialogue often tends to be split between students who take a theistic perspective versus those whose view is not informed by religion, but even so, it's been my experience that most students are willing to engage in dialogue with classmates who feel differently on the issue—and, in many ways, this is exactly what we hope for in doing philosophy with children.

LESSON PLAN: "WHY?"

Topic/Question

Meaning of Life/Why do anything?

Age Group

Kindergarten and up

Time

About thirty minutes

Materials

Tony Camp and Lindsay Ross, *Why?*

Description

This activity addresses a question that often comes up while students are wondering about life's meaning: "Why study philosophy?" The book *Why?* offers a suggestion that many people will find appealing: because asking questions—doing philosophy, essentially—can save the world.

Why? is a children's picture book about a girl named Lily who does one thing her father can't stand: she always asks, "Why?" She does it at breakfast, she does it when they go shopping, she does it at dinner, and, of course, she does it when she's called for bed. Usually, her father tries to answer her question, but sometimes, when he's tired, he just gets cranky. One day, though, something rather remarkable happens. Lily and her father are playing in the park, when a gigantic Thargon spaceship touches down and out squelch several Thargons; they don't look very friendly. "Tremble, Earthlings!" their leader cries. "We have come to destroy your puny planet." Everyone trembles, except Lily, who asks, "Why?" The Thargons don't have a good answer, and so they decide to return to the planet Tharg to think it over. That night, when Lily's father is tucking her in, he says how proud he was of her in the park and promises never to get angry when she asks "why?" ever again. Naturally, Lily asks him, "Why?" and the story ends there.

When reading this story to students, it's fun to stop regularly during the text and ask them questions, focusing especially on what sorts of claims they would like to ask "why?" about.

At the conclusion of the story, have students write down things they still wonder "why?" about at this point in the course. We do a fill-in-the-blank "poem" with this as the phrase to fill in: "After all this time, I still wonder why ____."

Some memorable responses from years past include the following:

- After all this time, I still wonder why I still wonder why.
- After all this time, I still wonder why there is no peace in the world.
- After all this time, I still wonder why school starts so early.
- After all this time, I still wonder why we study philosophy.
- After all this time, I still wonder why we don't know what happens when you die.
- After all this time, I still wonder why Dave won't stand on his head.

Pair up and discuss these remaining questions, and try to encourage students to keep wondering about them.

Remind them that, as Lily showed us, doing philosophy—asking "why?" again and again—really does have the potential to save the world.

EIGHT

Eleven Recommended Readings for Exploring Philosophy with Children

The standard model for conducting philosophy in sessions with children is to have students read aloud together some work of fiction that raises philosophical questions of one sort or another. Students then generate a list of questions from the text—those questions can be about anything, from specific questions about the story to broader, more "philosophical" inquiries. Questions are written on the board, often grouped thematically, then students choose—usually by voting—which questions they would like to take on. Discussion follows, using the questions students have expressed interest in.

Matthew Lipman and his colleagues at the Institute for the Advancement of Philosophy for Children (IAPC) have developed an entire curriculum of books to use when introducing children to philosophy. I have used all of the IAPC materials with some success, but working with them has encouraged me to seek out other readings, from the vast library of children's literature, that would have philosophical content, or at least would inspire philosophical inquiry. I've already mentioned a few of these, including E. B. White's classic *Stuart Little* and *Why?* by Tony Ross and Lindsay Camp.

In this section, therefore, I offer a short list of other such readings, with some comments about and suggestions for their use.

READING: LEWIS CARROLL, *ALICE IN WONDERLAND*, "A MAD TEA-PARTY"

Topic/Question

The Nature of Philosophy/What is philosophy?

Time

About forty-five minutes

Comments

Before explaining this exercise, it will be helpful to say a bit more about how readings are typically used in a philosophy class with kids.

As noted, philosophy for children, as an educational practice, has evolved primarily through the use of curriculum materials developed by the IAPC, which is a program connected to Montclair State University in Montclair, New Jersey. The materials, which include a collection of grade-specific stories written by Matthew Lipman as well as associated teacher's manuals, do an excellent job of raising philosophical questions for students of all ages. The original and most well-known of these stories is titled *Harry Stottlemeier's Discovery*, and it is designed to be used with students in grades 4–7 or so. Other volumes include *Pixie*, which is written for second and third graders, and *Lisa*, designed for ninth and tenth graders.

Harry follows the lives of a group of fifth or sixth graders who, both consciously and inadvertently, explore a number of questions in metaphysics, logic, epistemology, and ethics over the course of a school year.

Harry is divided into seventeen chapters, each of which can be used independently in one or more class periods. While each chapter tends to revolve around a single philosophical issue, the readings are richly textured enough that any number of interesting questions may arise from exploring them in a classroom situation.

The way the readings are typically employed is based on the encouragement of a classroom community of inquiry. Usually a chapter (or part of a chapter) is read aloud by students. All students are then given the opportunity to read a paragraph or two one after another. (Any student who prefers not to read aloud is permitted to simply indicate that he or she would like to pass.)

As the reading proceeds, students are encouraged to jot down any questions they have as a result of the material being read. What, in other words, do they wonder about as a result of what they're hearing?

At the conclusion of the reading, students share their questions with the entire class. There are several ways to do this. Sometimes the facilitator will ask students to present their questions consecutively. Another method is to break students into groups of two or three, have group members share their questions with each other, and then have each group decide which question or questions among them are most intriguing. Alternately, a facilitator might randomly call on students and pull questions from each student called upon.

Eventually, questions are written on the board, with the name of the student who asked each question following it. (It's common practice to include the name, especially with younger children. Fourth graders can be very proud of their questions; they like to see their names on the board with the questions they've asked.)

Once everyone who wants to share a question has had a chance to (or once the blackboard is completely full, or simply once time runs out), the class looks for common themes among the questions. Is it possible to group together any of the questions under a single idea? Usually it is, and it's valuable for students to be able to identify similarities among their questions. Indeed, just recognizing themes, seeing commonalities, and identifying shared points of inquiry is an important philosophical and critical thinking skill. Students who wonder together whether, say, the questions "Does time really exist?" and "Is there an end to the universe?" are getting at the same thing (as did students in a sixth-grade class) are doing metaphysics; they're inquiring into the nature of reality, whether they recognize it or not. In doing so, they are not only demonstrating their emerging philosophical acumen but also naturally entering into the long conversation that is the practice of philosophy. In many ways, this is plenty to accomplish in a philosophy lesson; should students succeed in generating questions and identifying common themes among them, a teacher can happily count the session as a success.

In any case, having identified common themes, students then choose which of the topics they would like to philosophize about first. There are several ways to do this, the most common of which is to have the class vote on their preferred question. (I usually make it a secret ballot; students have to close their eyes and raise their hands to cast their votes—this tends to reduce the peer pressure aspect.)

Alternately, the teacher might choose a student to decide which question to begin with. Or the questions can be numbered and chosen by random. What's key is that the teacher refrain from deciding; the choice should be driven by students in one way or another.

Classroom discussion then follows, starting with the winning question or questions. In this way, the topic and the approach to it has been generated by the class and so, in general, students tend to feel a sense of ownership of and interest in the issue or issues being explored.

In spite of (or perhaps because of) the simplicity of this process, it often produces quite lively discussions. It doesn't matter that the conversation isn't always what could be characterized as *always* deeply philosophical. Sometimes, for instance, students are more interested in questions about the story than the philosophical issues the story raises. They might want to spend a good deal of time talking about the behavior of the characters, or about whether the author of the story was on drugs when he wrote it. It's not uncommon for a discussion that begins as philosophically promising to become sidetracked in a session where kids are eager to recount experiences from their lives. While the facilitator will want to resist digressing completely from topics of philosophical interest and import and can take many steps to do so, he or she should also be aware that philosophy often springs up in unexpected ways. Consequently, it's worth it to trust the community of inquiry process and—as much as possible—allow students to drive and direct the discussion. By and large, the process is remarkably effective in eliciting discussion from students in classes of all sizes.

With that in mind, I turn back to *Alice in Wonderland*.

The selection we explore is the chapter titled "A Mad Tea-Party." Fans of Lewis Carroll will recall that this is the part of the story that is set up as follows:

> There was a table set out under a tree in front of the house, and the March Hare and the Hatter were having tea at it: a Dormouse was sitting between them, fast asleep, and the other two were using it as a cushion, resting their elbows on it, and talking over its head. (Lewis Carroll, *Alice in Wonderland*, 60)

The chapter is absurdly brilliant and raises all sorts of philosophical issues, including questions about the nature of time and the strangeness (and occasionally paradoxical quality) of logic, and issues related to morality, manners, and human sanity or insanity. The selection can be read aloud in a serial manner, with one student after another taking a paragraph or two, but it can be even more effective and interactive to assign the four characters in the scene (Alice, the Mad Hatter, the March Hare, and the Dormouse) to different students (I usually read the narration, but this can be assigned as well) and have them act out the scene, giving students the chance to mouth the very strange conversations taking place and providing an opportunity for their classmates to enjoy an odd and quite wonderful little "play."

A few passages usually elicit the most interest on the part of students. One of these is an exchange between Alice and the March Hare in which they debate whether it's the same thing to mean what one says and to say what one means. Typically, this can lead to a rich discussion with examples of each. For instance, one fifth-grade student explained that when he says what he means, it's intentional, like when he writes a paper for English class. But sometimes, he said, he can be surprised when he says what he means without quite intending to. A Freudian slip, for example, is a case of saying what you mean, even if you didn't mean to say it.

Another favorite topic of discussion is the running joke about a riddle the Mad Hatter asks: "Why is a raven like a writing desk?" Consider having students write down as many similarities as they can come up with. Responses I've heard include things like "they're both black," "both words start with the *r* sound," and "each can be sat upon." Sometimes one or more students are intent on knowing what the "correct" answer is. If so, take this as an opportunity to wonder together about what it would mean for an answer to a riddle to be correct. Is there really just one such answer? Would it have to be one that Lewis Carroll had in mind? What if there just isn't any such answer? Could there still be better or worse ones? (If students don't relent on the "correct answer" question, Cecil Adams's *Straight Dope* column provides some insight: http://www.straightdope.com/columns/read/1173/why-is-a-raven-like-a-writing-desk.)

Still another area that often inspires interest is an extended section in which the Hatter personifies time, and explains to Alice that if she kept on good terms with him (time), she could make him do whatever she wanted, including making the clock speed up whenever it was time for her school lessons to take place. Middle school students are especially intrigued by the philosophy of time and the various paradoxes associated with it. Simply raising the old philosophical chestnut about whether you could go back in time and kill your grandfather (thereby meaning you'd never have been born) is a tried-and-true way to get kids wondering about what time is and how it works.

In any case, here is a selection of questions that this section of *Alice in Wonderland* elicited from a group of fifth and sixth graders during the summer class of the year 2000:

- What happens to teatime when there is not tea?
- Is time controlled by a "someone"?
- If it were always six o'clock, wouldn't the characters be frozen?
- Do we really have an ability to control time?
- What is logical?
- Why *is* a raven like a writing desk?
- Has time stopped for everyone or just the characters at the table?
- What would happen if you gave a dormouse a cookie?

These students were especially interested in discussing the nature of time; more than half of the questions could be grouped thematically under that subject. So, when they voted on the topic they'd like to begin philosophizing about, the subject of time naturally won out.

The class was curious about the way in which time seems to speed up or slow down depending on what a person is doing. One girl, Kelsey, pointed out that the experience was quite paradoxical: When you wanted time to go quickly, it dragged. When you wanted it to stretch out, it zipped by.

We wondered together what this indicated. Did time really slow down? Or was it just that people wanted it to move more quickly? A boy named Noah said that thirty seconds standing on one foot certainly seemed longer than thirty seconds relaxing, even though he thought it was more fun to stand on one foot. That seemed odd to him because, usually, when he was doing something he liked, time would speed up.

A girl named Hannah brought the discussion back to the text. She wondered whether each of the characters was having a different experience of time. "Wouldn't it be moving much slower for Alice, who was being made fun of, than for the Dormouse, who was asleep?" she asked.

This led to a digression about how time is experienced when we're asleep and how strange it is that we can have dreams that seem to take hours but occur in just the space of seconds.

The discussion continued for about twenty minutes, and no definitive closure was reached. That is, the class didn't arrive at final answers to the questions they raised. Still, all of the students participated in the discussion and most seemed relatively satisfied with the nature of it.

Because so many students (at least when they first come to philosophy) want some sort of closure following discussions, it is a good practice to finish a philosophy lesson for children with some sort of activity that puts a "cap" on the session. With older students, a variety of techniques, such as pair-and-share writing, can be effective; with younger children, I often use a fill-in-the-blank "poem" to do this.

The "poem" that often follows from *Alice in Wonderland* is "One thing I've always wondered about is _____." Some recent answers from students are listed below:

- One thing I've always wondered about is whether the universe has an end.
- One thing I've always wondered about is why school starts so early.
- One thing I've always wondered about is what happens after we die.
- One thing I've always wondered about is what my life will be like in the future.
- One thing I've always wondered about is why people suffer.
- One thing I've always wondered about is how to make love last.

READING: MARGERY WILLIAMS, *THE VELVETEEN RABBIT*

Topic/Question

Metaphysics/What is real?

Age Group

Kindergarten and up

Time

About thirty minutes

Comments

The Velveteen Rabbit is a lovely story about a stuffed bunny and the boy who loves it. The story explores the metaphysical question "What is real?" The first chapter, which takes about ten minutes to read together in class, is sufficient to foster inquiry into the question, but I've also had success reading the entire book over several classes. One aspect of the story that's particularly "philosophical" is how there are different levels of "real," not unlike how Plato talks in *The Republic*.

For example, in the story, there are toys who pretend to be something they aren't really: a toy boat puts on airs and implies he is connected to government. Then there are toys that are just toys—they're not really the thing they purport to be; the rabbit, for instance, is just a toy rabbit. More real, however, are toys that have become "real" as a result of a child loving them: the boy in the story, for example, gets angry when his nurse says that the rabbit is a just a toy. "He's real!" cries the boy. Most real, however, are actual real things out in the world; at the conclusion of the story, for instance, the velveteen rabbit (who is "real" to the boy) is made into an actual living rabbit by the nursery fairy. Although it's not necessary to make explicit the connection to Plato when using this story, the similarities make for rich discussion in the classroom. An effective bookend to this lesson is to end with a fill-in-the-blank "poem" using the phrase "Something seems real to me when _____."

READING: BERNARD WISEMAN, *MORRIS THE MOOSE*

Topic/Question

Metaphysics/What makes something what it is?

Age Group

Pre-K through first grade

Time

About twenty minutes

Comments

Morris the Moose is a short picture book about Morris, a moose who thinks that every animal he meets is also a moose. For instance, Morris meets a deer and concludes that the deer is a moose since, like him, the deer has antlers on its head and four legs. As such, the story gets kids wondering about what makes something what it is. While reading the story aloud (it's especially effective with pre-readers), periodically stop and ask students what makes a moose a moose, or a deer a deer, or a cow a cow. In one class, students wondered together whether a deer could be a cat (no!), or a fish a rabbit (no!), or a sheep a dog (no, although one kid said, "Well, there *is* a sheepdog").

A typical ending to this lesson is to complete a fill-in-the-blank "poem" with the phrase "The difference between X and Y is _____," using the following list:

- The difference between a moose and a deer is _____.
- The difference between a cow and a fish is _____.
- The difference between lunch and dinner is _____.
- The difference between a deer and a horse is _____.
- The difference between a coyote and a dog is _____.
- The difference between a banana and a pineapple is _____.
- The difference between an otter and a moose is _____.
- The difference between a head and a foot is _____.
- The difference between Batman and Spiderman is _____.
- The difference between shoes and boots is _____.
- The difference between tables and chairs is _____.
- The difference between an easel and a desk is _____.
- The difference between fingers and toes is _____.
- The difference between a cow and a deer is _____.
- The difference between sitting and standing is _____.
- The difference between teeth and lips is _____.

READING: MADELEINE L'ENGLE, *A WRINKLE IN TIME,* "THE TESSERACT"

Topic/Question

Metaphysics/What is time?

Age Group

Fourth through seventh grade

Time

About thirty minutes

Comments

The chapter titled "The Tesseract" in *A Wrinkle in Time* is an excellent reading for exploring the concepts of time, time travel, and alternate dimensions. In it, the main character, a teenage girl named Meg Murry, along with her brother, a friend, and some other strange characters, travels to distant realms of the universe by moving through the fifth dimension. The reading usually spurs students to wonder whether such travel would indeed be possible and gets them pondering the difference between physical and logical impossibility, among other things. The section lends itself well to a "dramatic reading" of the text, where students assume the roles of the different characters in the story and read aloud just those parts. Conclude this lesson with a free-write in which students write their answers to the following fill-in-the-blank: "If I could travel anywhere in time or anyplace on earth, I would go to _____." They share these free-writes in pairs, then share them with the larger group.

READING: AMY GOLDMAN KOSS, *THE ASHWATER EXPERIMENT*

Topic/Question

Metaphysics/What is real?

Age Group

Fifth and sixth grade

Time

About thirty minutes

Comments

The Ashwater Experiment is the name of a thought experiment that twelve-year-old Hilary decides to try, where she imagines that every-thing that exists is just a figment of her imagination. The first chapter of the book lays out the thought experiment in vivid detail and gets students wondering about whether solipsism—the view that the only thing that exists in the universe is oneself—could be true. After exploring the questions that are raised by this reading, I like to have students imagine that they are the only thing that exists, and that everything else is a figment of their imagination. After entertaining this notion for a while and talking about it, we do a fill-in-the-blank "poem" using the following statement: "The way I know I'm not the only thing that exists is _____."

Here are a few sample answers from fifth graders:

- The way I know I'm not the only thing that exists is my little sister.
- The way I know I'm not the only thing that exists is because I could never invent all the stuff in the world.
- The way I know I'm not the only thing that exists is because of all the bad things that happen to people.
- The way I know I'm not the only thing that exists is because of my dog.

READING: J. K. ROWLING, *FANTASTIC BEASTS AND WHERE TO FIND THEM*

Topic/Question

Metaphysics/What makes something what it is?

Age Group

Fourth through sixth grade

Time

About twenty minutes

Comments

Fantastic Beasts and Where to Find Them is a mock-up of one of Harry Potter's textbooks from Hogwarts. Specifically, it is the classroom text for the Care of Magical Creatures class he is taking. The opening of the book has an excellent two-page essay on the history of classifying creatures as either beings or beasts and the various attempts made by officials of the magical world to do so. (A "being" is defined as a creature who has full standing as a member of the magical community, not unlike the term "person" when used in discussions about moral standing.) As such, this is a good introduction to the challenges of finding necessary and/or sufficient conditions for defining something. A lively follow-up to the reading is to have an in-class "debate" over a question that comes up in the reading: "Are Muggles (non-magical humans) beasts or beings?"

READING: FRANK L. BAUM, *THE TIN WOODMAN OF OZ*

Topic/Question

Metaphysics/Who or what am I?

Age Group

Fifth through seventh grade

Time

About thirty minutes

Comments

In chapter 18 of Frank L. Baum's *The Tin Woodman of Oz*, the Tin Woodman, on a quest to find his Munchkin sweetheart, Nimmie Ami, arrives at the shack of the Tinsmith, who made him. He goes poking around in various closets and, in one of them, finds a head that talks to him. It turns out that the head is his own former head, stashed there by the Tinsmith in the course of constructing the Tin Woodman. (The backstory that emerges in the conversation is that the Tin Woodman wasn't always tin; he was once a man but a jealous witch put a curse on his axe so that it kept chopping off parts of his body; the Woodman would then come to the Tinsmith to have the parts replaced with metal. The Tinsmith did so and then used the parts, along with some others from a tin soldier similarly afflicted by a cursed sword, to construct a third being, a so-called Ku-Klip, made up of a combination of spare parts from the other two.)

In any event, this reading raises all kinds of interesting questions about the nature of personal identity and who gets to claim to "really" be the Tin Woodman. There are five or six characters, so it lends itself pretty well to a staged reading. Wrap up the lesson by having students write down a minimum of six aspects of themselves that they think are essential to their personal identities. Working in pairs or trios, they then explore together whether any of the aspects are necessary and/or sufficient conditions of that identity and, by extension, whether any such conditions exist for any of us.

READING: FRANK TASHLIN, *THE BEAR THAT WASN'T*

Topic/Question

Metaphysics/How do I know who I am?

Age Group

Second through fifth grade

Time

About thirty minutes

Comments

The Bear That Wasn't is a picture book that tells the story of a bear that wakes up from hibernation one spring to discover that a factory has been built over his cave. He wanders out and is immediately set upon by the factory foreman and told to get to work. When the bear tries to explain that he is, in fact, a bear, the foreman laughs at him and says that no, he isn't; he is a silly man who needs a shave and is wearing a fur coat. Despite the bear's entreaties to the contrary, the foreman doesn't believe him and subsequently marches him through interviews with increasingly more powerful bosses in the factory, none of whom believe the bear.

Eventually, the bear concludes that he isn't a bear and, indeed, must be a silly man who needs a shave wearing a fur coat.

The story raises all sorts of questions about how we know what we know and whether, in the face of universal opposition, we would still be able to believe things about ourselves that no one else does.

End this lesson by having students do the following fill-in-the-blank "poem": "One thing about me that no one could ever convince me was false is _____."

READING: WILLIAM STEIG, *YELLOW AND PINK*

Topic/Question

Metaphysics/Does God exist?

Age Group

Fifth grade and up

Time

About thirty minutes

Comments

Yellow and Pink is a picture book that features a conversation between two figures made of wood, one of whom is yellow and the other of whom is pink. Together they ponder the question "How did we get here?" Yellow essentially articulates a scientific naturalistic position, explaining their creation via a series of "accidents" that resulted in the two figures' shapes, colors, and so forth. Pink is skeptical of this and opts for something more akin to the so-called design argument: he believes that the two figures are so well made that they must have had a designer.

Read this book aloud and ask questions as you proceed. For instance, at one point Yellow responds to Pink's skepticism by saying that the "accidents" took a long time to happen, maybe a million years. At that point, ask, "What could happen in a million years?" Students have responded with everything from "Humans could go extinct" to "The Seattle Seahawks could win the Super Bowl," the latter claim leading to one of the most lively and contentious discussions I've ever seen in a pre-college classroom.

READING: C. S. LEWIS, *THE LION, THE WITCH, AND THE WARDROBE*, CHAPTER 5

Topic/Question

Logic/What is truth?

Age Group

Fifth through seventh grade

Time

About twenty minutes

Comments

The fifth chapter in *The Lion, the Witch, and the Wardrobe* ("Back on This Side of the Door"), which comes right after the second time Lucy visits Narnia through the wardrobe, does a good job of raising questions about how logic works to establish true propositions. The older siblings are worried about their little sister's mental health, so they go and talk to the Professor about her. He creates for them a syllogism that yields the conclusion that the only logical explanation is that she is telling the truth.

The selection, which also lends itself well to a staged reading, usually leads to a discussion about what Lucy should believe and why. It's effective to pair this reading with the "How Many of These Do You Know to Be True?" list in chapter 2. Upon learning that only one of the propositions is indeed true, students can engage in a lively discussion about why they think claims that are false are true and what their criteria for knowledge are.

READING: CLAUDIA MILLS, *DINAH FOREVER*, CHAPTER 3

Topic/Question

Meaning of Life/What are we here for?

Age Group

Fifth through seventh grade

Time

About thirty minutes

Comments

Dinah Forever is the story of seventh-grade Dinah, who learns on the first day of school from her science teacher that our solar system will be consumed by the sun in something like five billion years. As a result, Dinah begins to wonder, "What's the point of doing anything? Why write poetry? Why recycle? Why try to be popular? If everything's eventually going to be destroyed by an exploding sun, why bother?"

The selection to read is chapter 3, where Dinah learns this fact. The last line of the text pretty much sums things up: "Footprints on the sands of time. Why should Dinah care if she left any, if in another five billion years—only five!—no one would know or care whether she had left any or not?"

This is the question to explore with students. Ponder it as a class and explore the question of what, if anything, is worth doing in light of humanity's eventual inevitable destruction. Rather heartwarmingly, it's not uncommon for students to take the position that among the things that remain worthwhile is philosophy!

Bibliography

Battin, Margaret, John Fisher, Ronald Moore, and Anita Silvers. *Puzzles about Art*. New York: St. Martin's, 1989.

Carroll, Lewis. *Alice's Adventures in Wonderland*. New York: Whittlesea, 1945.

Cohen, Martin. *101 Philosophy Problems*. New York: Routledge, 2002.

Lipman, Matthew. *Harry Stottlemeier's Discovery*. Montclair, NJ: First Mountain Foundation, 1974.

———. *Lisa*. Montclair, NJ: Institute for the Advancement of Philosophy for Children, 1983.

———. *Philosophy Goes to School*. Philadelphia: Temple University Press, 1988.

———. *Philosophy in the Classroom*. Montclair, NJ: Institute for the Advancement of Philosophy for Children, 1977.

———. *Pixie*. Montclair, NJ: Institute for the Advancement of Philosophy for Children, 1981.

———. *Thinking in Education*. New York: Cambridge University Press, 1991.

Lipman, Matthew, and Ann Margaret Sharp, eds. *Growing Up with Philosophy*. Philadelphia: Temple University Press, 1978.

Martin, Robert M. *There Are Two Errors in the the Title of This Book: A Sourcebook of Philosophical Puzzles, Problems, and Paradoxes*. Peterborough, Ontario: Broadview Press, 2002.

Matthews, Gareth. *Dialogues with Children*. Cambridge, MA: Harvard University Press, 1984.

———. *Philosophy and the Young Child*. Cambridge, MA: Harvard University Press, 1980.

———. *The Philosophy of Childhood*. Cambridge, MA: Harvard University Press, 1994.

Muth, Jon. *The Three Questions*. New York: Scholastic Press, 2002.

Paley, Vivian Gussey. *The Kindness of Children*. Cambridge, MA: Harvard University Press, 1999.

———. *You Can't Say You Can't Play*. Cambridge, MA: Harvard University Press, 1992.

Plato. *The Republic*. Translated by B. Jowett. New York: Modern Library, n.d.

Pritchard, Michael. *Reasonable Children: Moral Education and Moral Learning*. Lawrence: University Press of Kansas, 1996.

Rawls, John. *A Theory of Justice*. Cambridge, MA: Harvard University Press, 1971.

Sprod, Tim. *Philosophical Discussion in Moral Education: The Community of Ethical Inquiry*. New York: Routledge, 2001.

Wartenberg, Thomas. *Big Ideas for Little Kids: Teaching Philosophy through Children's Literature*. Lanham, MD: Rowman & Littlefield, 2009.

White, E. B. *Stuart Little*. New York: Harper and Row, 1945.